PUFFIN CANADA

RUNNING TO EXTREMES

STEVE PITT is a children's author and magazine writer whose non-fiction book *Rain Tonight: A Tale of Hurricane Hazel* was shortlisted for several Children's Choice Awards in Canada, including the Silver Birch Award. His novel *Faster Than Wind* was shortlisted for the Manitoba Young Readers Award. He lives in Rutherglen, Ontario.

STEVE PITT

WITH RAY ZAHAB

RUNNING TO EXTREMES

RAY ZAHAB'S AMAZING ULTRAMARATHON JOURNEY

PUFFIN
CANADA

PUFFIN CANADA

Published by the Penguin Group

Penguin Group (Canada), 90 Eglinton Avenue East, Suite 700, Toronto, Ontario, Canada M4P 2Y3
(a division of Pearson Canada Inc.)

Penguin Group (USA) Inc., 375 Hudson Street, New York, New York 10014, U.S.A.
Penguin Books Ltd, 80 Strand, London WC2R 0RL, England
Penguin Ireland, 25 St Stephen's Green, Dublin 2, Ireland (a division of Penguin Books Ltd)
Penguin Group (Australia), 250 Camberwell Road, Camberwell, Victoria 3124, Australia
(a division of Pearson Australia Group Pty Ltd)
Penguin Books India Pvt Ltd, 11 Community Centre, Panchsheel Park, New Delhi – 110 017, India
Penguin Group (NZ), 67 Apollo Drive, Rosedale, Auckland 0632, New Zealand
(a division of Pearson New Zealand Ltd)
Penguin Books (South Africa) (Pty) Ltd, 24 Sturdee Avenue, Rosebank, Johannesburg 2196,
South Africa

Penguin Books Ltd, Registered Offices: 80 Strand, London WC2R 0RL, England

First published 2011

1 2 3 4 5 6 7 8 9 10 (WEB)

Copyright © Steve Pitt, 2011

Manufactured in Canada.

LIBRARY AND ARCHIVES CANADA CATALOGUING IN PUBLICATION

Pitt, Steve, 1954–
    Running to extremes : Ray Zahab's amazing ultramarathon journey / Steve Pitt ; with Ray Zahab.

ISBN 978-0-14-317967-2

1. Zahab, Ray, 1969– —Juvenile literature. 2. Marathon running—Juvenile literature.
3. Runners (Sports)—Canada—Biography—Juvenile literature.
I. Zahab, Ray, 1969– II. Title.

GV1061.15.Z34P58 2011   j796.42'52092   C2011-902356-3

Visit the Penguin Group (Canada) website at **www.penguin.ca**

Special and corporate bulk purchase rates available; please see
www.penguin.ca/corporatesales or call 1-800-810-3104, ext. 2477 or 2474

For my wife, Kathy, our daughters, Mia Sahara and Anika Ixa, and fellow runner Patrick Doyle

—Ray Zahab

CONTENTS

ONE

LAST AGAIN

The cabin began to point downward almost as soon as the airliner had levelled off from its climb into the skies over Vancouver. Compared to the six-hour cross-country flight from Ontario to British Columbia, this connecting trip to Whitehorse, Yukon Territory, was going to be very short. Ray Zahab sat in his window seat and watched the mighty Rocky Mountains pass by below like so many snow-covered anthills.

"This is crazy," a voice said.

Ray ignored it. That was the Old Ray talking.

"It's freezing down there. Way below zero," the voice reminded him.

Ray tried to take no notice, but there was more than a little truth to what the Old Ray was saying. He was about to attempt something that would sound impossible to any sane person: running 160 kilometres (100 miles) through the Arctic snow at temperatures so cold that exposed skin could freeze in a matter of seconds. Even the thought of it made Ray's knees feel weak, but he had promised all his friends and family that he would try his very best to finish this race.

The crazy thing was that Ray wasn't even an experienced long-distance runner. But here he was, about to enter an ultramarathon, an event that would push even the most highly trained runners to their physical limits. An ordinary marathon race was impressive enough. Legend has it that twenty-five hundred years ago, a Greek soldier named Pheidippides ran 40 kilometres (25 miles) from a place in Greece called Marathon to the city of Athens to tell his countrymen that their army had triumphed in battle over a much larger Persian force. And as soon as he delivered his message he dropped dead from the strain!

Since then, marathon races have been the gold standard of long-distance racing. The marathon is traditionally the main event of the Olympics, and almost every major city in the world holds an annual marathon race. For most participants, finishing one of these races is an amazing accomplishment in itself. Ray's race would be three times as long, in snow and at temperatures that never rose above freezing.

But even a full marathon isn't the limit of human running endurance. People have been known to run more than twice a marathon's distance in one day, and sometimes they keep running extreme distances for several days in a row. These incredible races became known as ultramarathons. Originally, most ultramarathons were 50 or 100 kilometres (30 or 60 miles) long, but some eventually covered thousands of kilometres and took several weeks to complete.

Ultramarathons became extremely popular events in the nineteenth and early twentieth centuries. In the United States and Europe, "Six Day, Go As You Please" races were held in huge indoor stadiums like Madison Square Garden in New York City. Organizers made a fortune selling tickets to sports fans who would cheer their favourite competitors as they ran or walked as many laps as they could over the span of six days. The winners collected their share of the profits. In 1880, a Haitian-born African American by the name of Frank Hart won $17,000 for covering 909 kilometres (565 miles) in six days.

Other races were sponsored by publishers to sell newspapers or by sports promoters who sold souvenir books, trinkets and foot ointments to the tens of thousands of spectators who lined the route. In 1927, Lon Scott, an American sports promoter, organized a race across the United States, from Los Angeles to New York City, to celebrate the opening of Route 66, the first highway to span North America from coast to coast. First prize was $25,000, which was a tremendous fortune at the time. Despite the hefty $100 entrance fee, the race attracted nearly three hundred athletes from around the world, including Britain's Arthur F.H. Newman, Canada's Phillip Granville and Finland's Nestor Erickson, who were among the most famous runners of the day. More than seventy racers quit the first day, and by the end of the first week, the field had narrowed to just 145. Despite the star-studded competition, it was Andy Payne, a twenty-year-old First Nations man from Oklahoma, who won the race, completing the 5,507-kilometre (3,422-mile) course in 573 hours, 4 minutes and 34 seconds, or almost twenty-four days.

By the 1930s, however, Sunday afternoon sporting events such as professional baseball, hockey, football, boxing and basketball had begun to overshadow long-distance-running events, which often took days or even weeks to complete. The remarkable prize money dried up, and only the dedication of a few hundred extreme runners around the world kept the sport alive. Ultramarathon races transformed from money events to personal challenges.

Anyone is welcome to try an ultramarathon, but few people can endure the hardships of running such long distances day after day. Some races take place over a series of days; some are run in both daytime and nighttime conditions. Many ultramarathons are held in extreme locations, like mountain ranges and deserts, the Arctic tundra and tropical rainforests. A few runners have even completed the ultramarathon grand slam, which means they have competed on all seven continents and at both poles.

One of the most famous modern ultramarathons is the Yukon Arctic Ultra. This race was inspired by another endurance event—the Yukon Quest, which is the world's longest, hardest dogsled race. For thousands of years, dogsleds were the traditional way for First Nations people to travel long distances in the North. When snowmobiles replaced dog teams for northern work duties, some people still kept their dogs and ran them for sport. Today, the best teams and drivers in the world gather in the city of Fairbanks, Alaska, and race more than 1,600 kilometres (about a thousand miles) to Whitehorse, Yukon Territory. The race is held in February, when temperatures routinely plummet to –40 degrees at night and the daylight is limited to only a few hours. Participants have to carry all their supplies in their sleds, including food, fuel for cooking, a camp stove and some sort of shelter to sleep in during rest stops. The race is challenging not just for its distance and extreme conditions but also for its isolation. Once the field has spread out, racers can go for hours or days without seeing another person.

The Yukon Arctic Ultra follows the same route, but it runs in the opposite direction, from Whitehorse to Fairbanks. Runners have to follow almost the same rules as the Yukon Quest competitors, except that they don't have the help of a dog team. They have to carry their own supplies through the snow.

Many seasoned Ultra runners have thousand-dollar sleds and the best professional equipment money can buy. But Ray was on a much more modest budget. As he thought about his homemade sled and lack of experience, his optimism wavered. "Just let me finish this race," he told himself. "I need to finish something."

As the airliner began its final descent into Whitehorse, Ray's mind wandered back to his high school days. Like most young teens, he'd often felt awkward and out of place, but in gym class, Ray's insecurities were especially amplified. Gym class was a source of constant humiliation for him because no matter what sport was to be played, he was almost always the last guy chosen for the team. It's not that Ray wasn't athletic: he'd been raised on a farm, and could run and ride a horse better than most people he knew. But skills like that didn't seem to matter in his high school in the Ottawa suburb of Kanata, Ontario.

All high school sports seemed to involve a ball of some sort that people had to catch, hit, toss through a hoop or launch at another classmate. These were sports that town kids had grown up with all their lives. Give Ray a horse and he could ride rings around his classmates, but throw him a ball and he'd miss it, drop it or catch it with his face.

Although he hid it well, Ray was deeply affected by the constant humiliation he endured in gym class. It made him think very little of himself, and his lack of self-esteem affected his performance in other classes. Rather than risk trying for good grades and failing, Ray adopted the mask of a person who just didn't care how he did in school. He became known as one of those happy-go-lucky students who never hope for much out of life, and he got exactly what he expected. Like most guys his age, he was shy around girls, especially those who seemed to gravitate toward the boys who were good at sports or did well in other ways.

Ray didn't have any long-term goals. He envied classmates who, even as high school students, seemed to know what they wanted to do with the rest of their lives. Some were going to be teachers or doctors. Others were going into their parents' small-town businesses. Ray thought only that maybe he wanted to be a horse trainer ... or something. Because it seemed like a cool thing to do, he took up smoking at the age of fourteen. Then he began to sneak the occasional beer behind his parents' backs. Cigarettes and beer soon became the focal point of having a good time with his friends. After a few beers, the awkwardness slipped away and Ray felt good for a while.

When Ray turned sixteen, he immediately got his driver's licence. He became interested in fast cars and rebuilt a four-speed 1969 Camaro he bought off a neighbour. The car was both a positive and a negative influence on Ray. To buy gas and new parts, he had to act responsibly—at least long enough to earn money from part-time work. Unfortunately, he also liked to drive very fast, and by the age of seventeen he had already lost his driver's licence temporarily for speeding.

After high school Ray applied to study business administration at Algonquin College in Ottawa. He wasn't really interested in business, but he wasn't sure what else to do with his life. At college, Ray's bad habits began to take over more of his life. He sometimes smoked two packs of cigarettes a day, and he often missed classes and even whole days of studies because he'd been up all night drinking beer and partying with his college buddies. Then a series of family tragedies sent his life into a real tailspin.

All his life, Ray had known his grandfather as an active man full of energy. Suddenly, lung cancer reduced this vibrant man into a frail walking skeleton, killing him in a matter of months. Ray could not comprehend how a person could seem perfectly healthy one day and be so ill the next. Then, almost a year to the day of his grandfather's death, Ray's uncle Tom was killed in a farm accident when the tractor he was driving rolled over and crushed him. Once again, a major figure in Ray's life was taken from him without warning.

Ray barely had time to deal with the unexpected loss of both his grandfather and his uncle when his father suffered a severe stroke. Before the stroke, Ray's father had been a cheerful, active person who lived life to its fullest. He was a surgeon who saved people's lives, and he was very involved in the community. Now he had to struggle to complete the simplest tasks.

Up until then, Ray had always thought that life was about having fun. Smoking, drinking and driving too fast were just his way of passing the time, and there seemed to be no real consequences to his actions. But after these three misfortunes, he began to think that life was about losing the things that are most precious to you. His grandfather, uncle and father had done nothing to deserve their awful misfortunes, yet it seemed to Ray that fate took a personal delight in striking them down. He lost interest in school. He didn't complete his business diploma. He dropped out and drifted from one occupation to another.

Ray tried starting a landscaping business. After a while he lost interest in it and took up training horses. Although he discovered that he loved training horses, he felt as if he was just spinning his wheels. He had visions of himself forty years down the road, still working for other people and driving his '69 Camaro. Ray tried to drown his unhappiness in beer and cigarettes, but it dawned on him one day that life wouldn't get better on its own. He had to take charge of his own fate.

Fortunately, Ray had a role model to look up to—his younger brother, John. Like him, John had been a heavy smoker in his teens, but in 1996 he quit cigarettes and became an outdoor athlete. John was an expert at trail hiking and mountain biking. Ray began to accompany his brother on these strenuous outings, but the cigarettes and beer took their toll. He often had to stop on the trail to catch his breath. John would wait patiently for him, but Ray realized that he had to choose between his brother's way of life and the cigarettes. He had tried quitting smoking on a couple of occasions in the past, but he'd always slipped back into his old bad habits.

By coincidence, the year 2000 was approaching. January 1 would mark not only a new year but also a new century and a new millennium. This struck Ray as the perfect time to create a new Ray. Although he dabbled in some of John's adventures, he kept smoking right up until midnight of December 31, 1999. He passed the last few seconds of the old year, old century and old millennium with a cigarette in his mouth. As his friends and family counted down 1999 with a "three ... two ... one ..." and shouted "Happy New Year!" Ray extinguished his final cigarette. The year 2000 looked and felt exactly like 1999 to everyone around him, but there was a new road ahead for Ray.

TWO

FROM COLD TURKEY TO COLD TOOTSIES

Quitting smoking was exactly what Ray had expected it to be—unpleasant at first, but no worse than getting over a bad flu or a case of measles. He'd never realized that he possessed the mental power to force his body to ignore its nicotine cravings. And Ray's new lifestyle had other pleasant surprises. Food suddenly smelled and tasted better. He found he had more energy than before, and his endurance improved. His outlook on life even improved—he realized that his addiction to tobacco had made him feel edgy and depressed. He was smoking cigarettes not to feel better but just to feel normal. As Ray shook off his addiction, his natural optimism returned.

"Quitting smoking is 90 percent mental," he liked to say, "and the other 10 percent is all in my head." But he found that the last 10 percent was a hundred times harder than the first 90. That's where all the self-doubts and easy excuses lurked. And sometimes, a voice in the back of his head nagged him for a cigarette.

"Only one," the voice pleaded. "What harm could one cigarette do?" But that was the Old Ray talking. The New Ray knew that there was no such thing as "only one" cigarette. He ignored the voice, and each day the cravings became fainter and fainter. For the first time in years, Ray felt as if his mind was in full control of his body, instead of the other way around.

His newly energized body began longing for physical challenges again—the kind he'd enjoyed back in his days on the farm. He continued to take pleasure in mountain biking and hiking with his brother, only now he could keep up and sometimes even challenged John to go faster and farther. To test their skills and endurance, they scrambled up the toughest local forest trails they could find. When winter came, they used ice axes and foot spikes called crampons to climb frozen waterfalls in the Calabogie Hills near Ottawa.

These highly physical activities were completely unlike the high school sports that had left Ray feeling so hopelessly inadequate. There were no captains, no stars, no teams, no winners or losers. There was only you, challenging yourself to do better. Ray found that mountain biking and extreme hiking were similar to quitting smoking—90 percent mental, with the other 10 percent all in his head—but once again, the last 10 percent was the hardest part. In every outing there came a point when Ray felt as if his lungs were going to explode or his legs were going to melt. But he kept pushing, and he found he could go on and do better. Each time he set a new personal record hiking or biking, Ray felt a sense of real accomplishment.

One day, on a routine visit to his chiropractor's office, he happened to see a magazine called *Explore*. *Explore* bills itself as "Canada's Outdoor Magazine" because its articles are about people who like to challenge themselves by doing very physical things. In the issue Ray picked up, there was an article about a man who'd climbed the steepest and most dangerous side of a very high mountain, and another about a woman who'd paddled a kayak down canyons full of rushing whitewater. The article that really caught Ray's attention, however, was about a race whose partici- pants ran non-stop for 160 kilometres (100 miles) in the middle of a Yukon winter. The idea struck Ray as crazy—so crazy he knew he just had to try it.

The problem was that Ray wasn't an experienced runner. He'd never even run a half marathon, let alone an ultramarathon. But "never" was the Old Ray way of thinking. The New Ray began considering the assets he did have and thinking about how he could turn those assets into racing advantages.

For one, Ray's health had improved considerably since he'd quit smoking and drinking. He had even competed in a couple of mountain bike races, posting better times than many professional athletes at their own sport. But Ray rarely thought about beating other racers. In every race he concentrated on beating his personal best time. To him, the other athletes were just comrades enduring the same challenges. Ray's competitiveness was focused against just one person: the Old Ray.

One other advantage was that Ray now lived in the village of Chelsea, Quebec. By coincidence, quite a few athletes lived in this small town, and Ray had no trouble finding experienced marathon runners who generously agreed to share their knowledge with him. Whenever they found out that Ray intended to run the Yukon Arctic Ultra for his first race, they would shake their heads and say, "You're crazy!" He would just smile and say, "I know," and continue to ask his questions anyway.

Ray had only a few months to prepare. Pat Doyle, a good friend who was also an experienced runner, offered to take him on an eight-kilometre (five-mile) loop around a local highway to show him how to run. It was mid-December in 2003. There wasn't much snow on the ground yet, but the temperature was already below freezing. Despite the cold, both runners dressed lightly, with just double-layer tights and jackets over their T-shirts and long underwear. As they started running, Pat gave Ray advice on how to pace himself. "Breathe! Watch your stride. Relax!" he called out as cars whizzed by them on the highway.

On that first day, Ray had trouble completing the full distance. At the six-kilometre (3.7-mile) point, pain and fatigue took over. He slowed to a walking pace but didn't stop until he finished the run. It wasn't a pretty end, but finishing the course made him feel as if he had accomplished something. The next day, Ray attempted the run on his own. This time he finished without having to walk. On his third run he added four extra kilometres (2.5 miles) and finished them, too. Soon he was running four or five times a week and extending his range dramatically. As his distances increased, he was sometimes forced to walk for part of his journey. But he never gave up on a run before he completed the full distance.

When he wasn't training, Ray was carefully assembling his Yukon running kit. By coincidence, his landlord was Richard Weber, the first man to cross-country ski to the North Pole. Richard willingly shared his knowledge of Arctic conditions and advised Ray on what kind of equipment he'd need to survive as he ran in such an unforgiving environment.

He told Ray to get a small backpack to hold essentials and also a small sled to tow behind him to carry his sleeping bag, food and stove. His clothes had to be ultra-light and yet warm enough to help him survive the below-freezing temperatures. Ray had noticed that some runners used ski poles to help them climb up hills and pull their sleds, and he decided the poles were a good idea. He also had to figure out a way to keep his water from freezing. An Arctic runner needs at least two litres (four pints) of liquid water to get through a day's running, and the longer the run, the more chance the water has to freeze. Ray wrapped two separate water bottles in lightweight foam that he hoped would keep them warm enough if they were next to his body in his backpack.

On the Internet, Ray had found a lightweight stove that used solid fuel that wouldn't freeze or leak if it got bumped on the trail. And he saw many other wonderful things. If he'd had unlimited money, he would have been able to pull together his Yukon Arctic Ultra ensemble in a matter of hours. Unfortunately, Ray was still living on a very tight budget. He was eager to share what he was learning about fitness and had started a personal-training business to do so. So far, customers were scarce, and with not much money coming in, he had only a few hundred dollars to spend on Arctic running equipment.

But one thing Ray did have was an ability to improvise. He studied the professional ultramarathon sleds offered online and decided that he could modify a ten-dollar kid's sled from a local department store. He bolted sturdy eyelets to the front of the sled to attach a hauling harness and built a plastic cover to fit over it to prevent his equipment and supplies from falling out as he crossed the rugged terrain. When they heard about Ray's crazy plan, some local Chelsea merchants offered to be his sponsors. A law firm gave him some money to purchase his plane tickets and to cover expenses like meals and hotel accommodations. Greg Christie, who owned a local bike shop, gave Ray some warm and lightweight racing clothes.

Piece by piece and precious nickel by nickel, Ray assembled his Arctic kit. He went running with it and discovered its flaws, rebuilt it and tried it again. He trained six days a week. On Mondays, Wednesdays, Saturdays and Sundays, he went running early in the morning over hilly ski trails. On Tuesdays and Thursdays, he stretched out his legs on a stationary bike.

Finally it was time to fly to the Yukon. From his mountain biking experience, Ray knew that competitors often had a hard time picking out their kit bags from dozens of similar ones at the airport. As a private joke to himself, he spray-painted a big skull and cross-bones on the plastic tub that contained his equipment before he checked it in with the airline. Fifteen hours later, he was in Whitehorse. Compared to the Ottawa and Vancouver airports, the Whitehorse terminal looked more like a bus station. The big airliner they had just arrived on was the only one sitting on the runway, and barely a hundred people were in the terminal.

A crowd of people, many of them obviously racers, stood by the luggage carousel. Suitcases, duffle bags, bicycles, skis and other sports equipment came tumbling down the chute like a slow avalanche. One by one, the pieces were picked up until there was only an empty merry-go-round. Ray stood there for five more minutes, but no more luggage appeared.

With a sinking feeling, he walked to the ticket counter.

"My luggage didn't come down the chute," he said.

"Can you describe it?" the airline attendant asked.

"Yeah, it's a big plastic box with a skull and cross-bones painted on it," Ray answered.

The attendant looked at him as if he was trying to decide if Ray was serious or being a jerk. Settling on the former, he said he would do the best he could to find his luggage.

For most travellers, lost luggage is just an inconvenience. In time, the majority of lost bags are found, and the unlucky few can easily replace a bag full of socks and underwear. But Ray's baggage included specialized gear that had taken months to assemble. The race started in less than twenty-four hours, and it wouldn't be delayed just because one runner's kit hadn't arrived. If his luggage wasn't found in time, he wouldn't be able to compete. All his training, all the money spent and all the support from his friends and family would have been for nothing.

But there wasn't anything Ray could do except find his hotel and wait. "Don't panic. It will be fine," he told himself.

"I told you so," the Old Ray said.

By the time Ray climbed aboard the shuttle bus to the hotel, he found he was already a local legend.

"Are you the guy who lost his luggage?" a British woman asked as he took his seat. She made it sound as if it were his fault.

"Yep, that's me," Ray said.

"How many races have you run before?" the man beside her asked.

"None," Ray said. "But I'm going to give it a try!"

The two Brits looked at Ray as if he were completely out of his mind, but then they smiled, and Ray couldn't help laughing. The woman introduced herself as Shirley Thompson. The man sitting beside her was her husband, Mike. Ray didn't know it at the time, but this was the beginning of one of the many long-term friendships he'd form in the running community.

At the hotel, there were racers from all over the world milling around and chatting. Many were old friends and rivals who had competed against one another many times. Even though he was completely new to this sport, Ray felt immediately at home among all the experienced runners. They offered him tips and encouragement. Later that evening, the race organizers held a pre-race briefing, where they went over the course and the problems competitors might encounter. They spoke about the two biggest dangers in the race: frostbite and hypothermia. With frostbite, parts of the human body freeze as solid as a piece of meat in the freezer. Any body part that gets that frozen, like a nose or some toes, might have to be amputated, which would leave the runner lame or disfigured for life. And hypothermia is even worse. There, the whole body gets so cold it slowly shuts down from the outside in. If the runner doesn't manage to warm up somehow, he or she will die.

Ray was just digesting the image of himself without a nose or being found face down in a snowbank like a human popsicle when he received some good news— his gear had been located and it was on its way to the hotel. He was back in the race!

Although he desperately needed to rest, Ray was so keyed up about the race that he found he couldn't sleep that night. He left his room and met two other runners with the same problem. Together, they spent the night sorting their gear and getting ready for the race.

The Yukon Arctic Ultra is really several races in one. It has three finish lines. You can race a regular marathon of 42 kilometres (26 miles), an ultramarathon of 160 kilometres (100 miles), or the full 360 kilometres (224 miles). You can race on cross-country skis, on foot or on a bicycle. You can do it in teams of two or by yourself. Each distance and mode of racing has its advantages and disadvantages. The skiers and cyclists have an edge when the trail is flat, for example, but the runners have the advantage when the course begins to go up and down steep hills.

No matter what distance people were planning to run, everyone started at the same place and same time, at some railroad tracks that ran parallel to the Yukon River north toward Dawson City. At the starting line, there were hundreds of people milling around—well-wishers, curious local Yukoners and media people with cameras and microphones. Some of the well-known runners were being interviewed as if they had already completed the race.

Despite his lack of sleep, Ray was raring to go. The sub-zero temperatures made the hairs in his nose stick together and his breath come out in steamy puffs, but Ray felt perfectly comfortable.

Suddenly there was silence as the racers hunkered down at the starting line. Everyone in the whole territory seemed to hold their collective breath. The starter's pistol went *bang!* and all the runners, cyclists and skiers began moving forward, with hundreds of spectators cheering them on.

The first kilometre (half a mile) was like running in a stampeding herd, as everyone kept up and ran at the same basic pace. By the fifth kilometre (third mile), however, the herd had begun breaking up into bunches and long lines of single runners. The race organizers had arranged a mandatory checkpoint just past the 40-kilometre (25-mile) mark; all racers had to stop there and check their gear. Ray made it his first-day goal just to reach that checkpoint without dropping out.

Ray was lightly dressed for sub-zero weather, but the exertion of running while towing his small homemade sled was more than enough to keep him warm. Like a human steam engine, he puffed out his breath in regular blasts, and his arms and legs pumped like pistons, keeping up a steady rhythm.

As long as the race route paralleled the railroad tracks, the ground stayed pretty level and it was easy going. But as the racers neared the first checkpoint, the route swung away from the tracks and Ray saw a huge hill looming in front of him. Most of the skiers and bikers had to dismount to climb the hill. Many looked ready to quit already. Fortunately, all the training he'd done with John in the Gatineau and Calabogie Hills had prepared Ray for this type of climbing. He kept chugging along, with his sled bouncing behind him like a little caboose.

As he reached the crest of the hill, the smell of coffee pricked his nostrils. Just beyond the check-in tables was a large hospitality tent. Inside were sandwiches and hot drinks for the ultramarathoners to enjoy while the organizers checked over their gear to make sure they were properly equipped to continue the race. A large number of competitors—those doing the regular 42-kilometre (26-mile) run—were congratulating one another on their respective times. For them, the race was over. But Ray had barely begun.

THREE

CHECKING IN AND OUT OF REALITY

Most people would be looking for the nearest warm bed after running a full sub-zero marathon, but Ray and all the other ultramaratho-ners couldn't even sit down for a decent coffee break. Each one had to unpack his or her kit bag and set up a temporary camp so that race organizers could see if the runner had suitable clothes, a sleeping bag and a working camp stove with sufficient fuel and food. Most runners carried their gear in a "bivy bag," which is a large lightweight sack that a runner could even use as a temporary shelter for a quick nap. The runner could climb in, clothes and all, curl up in his or her sleeping bag and close the bivy bag, leaving just a small opening near the face for breathing.

Runners were required to spend exactly four hours at the checkpoint while their gear was examined. To satisfy the race organizers, each one had to light his or her stove and melt enough snow in a pan to make a decent drink or mix a dehydrated meal pack. Ray had assembled a camp stove before, but this was the first time he'd had to do it wearing thick gloves. It was like trying to light a lamp wearing boxing gloves. The gloves made everything hard to hold, but if he took them off, the sub-zero temperatures would cause his hands to freeze up in seconds. With perseverance and semi-numb fingers, Ray eventually lit his stove and melted the snow in the pan. Now he had to repack his sled and get ready to resume the race. Once their gear was cleared, runners could leave whenever they wanted to. Some took a little extra time to catch up on sleep. Others, like Ray, left as soon as they could to maintain their position in the race.

A more experienced Yukon runner named Rob finished his checkout at the same time as Ray, so they decided to run the next leg of the race together. The Ultra is always held in the second week of February, when the weather is coldest and the days are shortest. Even though it was only mid-afternoon, the sun was already beginning to set by the time Rob and Ray trekked down to the racing trail by the Yukon River, which was the next starting point. Ray was grateful for Rob's company because running alone at night could be very lonely.

Getting lost at night in the Yukon wilderness could be fatal, so racers wore lightweight LED (light-emitting diode) lights strapped to their heads as they ran. The glow of the northern lights and thousands of stars reflected eerily off the forest snow as they ran. It was like jogging in a surreal twilight that was not quite nighttime, but they still had to keep sharp to spot the brightly coloured trail marks spray-painted into the snow by race organizers.

Ray was beginning to find his stride. Instead of fighting the snow by trying to push through it with brute force, he tried to pick his way along where he could see the going was easier. He kept his back straight, which helped him to be more relaxed, and took shorter strides for better traction.

After several more hours, Ray noticed that Rob's running was beginning to look a bit ragged. He stumbled frequently and wobbled from side to side now and then. "Are you all right?" Ray asked, but Rob shrugged off his concerns with a wave and a determined smile.

As the stumbling and weaving got worse, Ray began to suspect that Rob was driving himself on despite the warning signals that he was hungry and thirsty. In ultramarathons, one of the biggest challenges is to keep hydrated. Precious bodily fluids are lost as the runner's body perspires. This happens at sub-zero temperatures just as much as it does in a heat wave. When you're running in warm or even moderate temperatures, it's easy to remember to drink fluids because your mouth dries up and you feel thirsty. But at $-20°C$ ($-4°F$), the cold air makes your throat burn, and that masks the feeling of thirst. Dehydration can easily occur.

In an Arctic winter race, finding drinking water can also be time-consuming. The Yukon Arctic Ultra wasn't like a normal marathon race, where volunteers at stations along the course hand runners cups of water to slug down on the run. Out here, the runners were completely on their own. They could carry their own drinking water in bottles, but after a few hours, the bottles would freeze. To keep from dehydrating, runners would then be forced to stop, unpack their stoves and melt snow to drink. All this took precious time, and many runners were reluctant to sacrifice that time for a mere drink of water.

Besides having the two insulated water bottles in his pack, Ray scooped and swallowed small handfuls of snow to cool his throat on the way. But Rob doggedly pressed on without drinking any water or eating any snow. As Ray had often told himself, extreme sports are all about ignoring the pleading inner voices pressing you to give in to a craving for something your body wants but really doesn't need. At the same time, part of that last 10 percent of competing was knowing the difference between a whiny craving and an actual bodily need.

Rob's pace slowed down until they were finally just walking. He confessed to Ray that he'd been too excited about the run to even eat, so he was not only dehydrated but also operating on an empty stomach. Ray offered him some power bars, but Rob was too groggy to eat more than a few bites. As they walked their bodies began to cool, and Ray started to worry that he was going to catch a chill.

The situation was now officially dangerous. Ray and Rob weren't in the middle of a city, or even in rural farmland where help was fairly close by. They were alone in the middle of the Yukon wilderness, in below-freezing temperatures. And they were still 20 kilometres (12 miles) from the next checkpoint. If they strayed off the race trail at all, it could be hours or even days before they saw another person. Rob knew that if Ray stayed with him they would both be in trouble, so he insisted that Ray resume running. Ray was reluctant but finally agreed, promising to send help back as soon as he could.

He suddenly felt very alone. It was dark and he was now very tired. And when you're tired, cold and hungry, your mind can start to play tricks on you. As the trail wound up and down several steep hills, Ray actually began to hallucinate. He imagined that he could see stairs running up and down the hills. He was so tired, in fact, that he actually felt himself falling asleep on his feet. He knew that running while half conscious wasn't a smart thing to do—he could easily get lost, hit a tree or a rock, or hurt or kill himself in at least a hundred other ways. So as much as he hated to take a break, he knew he was risking a lot more than losing a race if he kept on running.

Ray's running slowed down to a walk and then his walk slowed to a complete halt. He sat down on his sled and took stock of his situation. "I hate this," he admitted. He thought of his friends and family back home. He'd promised all those people he would do his very best. He heard a voice say, "How do I get out of this?" It was the Old Ray talking again. The Old Ray began finding lots of excuses he could give his friends and family for not finishing the race. "It was just too cold. Too long. Too rough. My water froze. That other guy slowed me down." The people back home would believe him, Ray knew. They had no idea what it was like out here.

But Ray knew there was no fooling himself. Every day for the rest of his life, he would have to face himself and ask, "Did you really do your very best?" Every day for the rest of his life, he knew the answer would be no. "You could have kept going, but you didn't. When the going got tough, you quit." He took a deep breath. He knew he had to keep running until he either finished the race or was found frozen in the snow from trying. But he allowed himself one concession: he decided to take a quick nap.

To keep his bearings, Ray pointed his ski poles in the direction of the next checkpoint. Then he dumped out his bivy bag and climbed in, still wearing his shoes, jacket and even headlamp. He set his wrist-watch alarm for two minutes and fell asleep in less than a heartbeat. *Weep-weep! Weep-weep!* The tiny alarm woke him up again almost immediately. Ray still felt tired and cold, but at least now he could keep going without hitting the trees on the trail. He climbed out of his bivy bag, quickly repacked his sled and resumed running. The dawn was breaking. The pale Arctic sun gave an illusion of warmth, and even that helped to raise Ray's spirits.

For the next few hours, Ray didn't think about the finish line or even the next checkpoint. He thought only about the moment he was in. He would pick out a tree ahead and run to it. Then he would pick out a stream ahead and run to that. "Just to that rock. Just to that stick," Ray kept telling himself as he devoured the race course one tiny bite at a time.

When he reached the next checkpoint, he immediately told them about Rob. He was relieved to hear that he had already been picked up by one of the race patrols. Ray noticed that the race organizers seemed surprised to see him. When he asked why, they said that although some skiers had already checked in, Ray was the first runner they'd seen.

He didn't quite believe the news. At the beginning of the race, many runners had pulled ahead of him and eventually disappeared from view. He had passed quite a few over the hours, but he couldn't believe he'd pulled into the lead. Was he really in first place? Just the possibility of finishing the race as he had hoped charged him with new energy.

Ray's feet now seemed to kick through the snow on their own power. The terrain also began to change to his advantage. Except for those few hills where he'd hallucinated, the race course had mostly been flat, which had favoured the skiers in the race. Now bigger, steeper hills appeared. As he fought up and down hill after hill, Ray began to pass skiers who were struggling against gravity with their suddenly cumbersome equipment.

His body had found its own inner rhythm. He didn't have to think about running anymore—his body just mechanically put one foot in front of the other and kept moving on its own. Ray's mind was free to think about other things. He thought about Braeburn Lodge, the place that marked the finish line. He'd heard they were world famous for their huge cinnamon rolls, and he promised his stomach a dozen of them when the race was over. He thought too about his friends and family back home, and how amazed they would be if they could see him running in the Arctic snow. But most of all, he dreamed about finishing the race.

At the 130-kilometre (80-mile) mark, Ray came to the third and final checkpoint. As soon as he stopped running, his head began to ache and his legs felt like jelly. Ray believed that if he sat down or even stood still for a few seconds too long, his body would crumple like wet cardboard. He paused only long enough to fill up his water bottles before he launched himself back into the wilderness for the long final leg of the run.

The trail was an endless roller coaster of hills now. Every joint in Ray's body seemed to be on fire as he doggedly moved forward through the ever-deepening snow. His water soon froze, and once again he was forced to hydrate himself with handfuls of snow. He thought he was hallucinating all over again when he saw a man standing on the trail with a TV camera. But he wasn't hallucinating—it was a news reporter. The man asked Ray how he was feeling. Every bone in Ray's body screamed out that it was broken, and every muscle felt like mush. "I feel great!" he lied, and the reporter nodded and smiled.

Ray was almost at the finish line now. He had only to cross frozen Braeburn Lake and run up to the lodge. But one of the experienced runners had warned Ray that the last ten kilometres (six miles) were the hardest. You could see the lodge for a long distance, which gave you hope, but then you hit a series of steep hills that seemed deliberately designed to break the heart of the most determined racers.

"Don't work so hard," murmured a voice in Ray's head "You're going to finish for sure. You can afford to slack off and walk." Only three kilometres (less than two miles) to go and the Old Ray was back. Ray jammed his feet even harder into the snow. The pain made the Old Ray go away. The lodge was getting so close now that his eyes could make out the green roof and brown wooden porch. There was a light on over the steps, and Ray could see a banner with just one beautiful word: "Finish." He thought he could smell cinnamon and french fries.

Ray's foot hit the front porch. He was finished! He looked around. The parking lot was half full of cars, but there wasn't a soul to be seen. It was dead silent. He hadn't expected a big fanfare, but this seemed a bit low-key even for the middle of the Yukon wilderness. Was he at the real finish line? Where was everybody?

Ray stepped through the front doors of the lodge. There were several people sitting at a table. Many of them had tags that identified them as race organizers. They looked up at him as if he were just another tourist.

"I'm done," Ray said.

"What? You racers are here already?" someone asked incredulously.

"No. Just me," Ray said.

"How'd you get here?" another staffer asked.

"I ran."

Ray couldn't understand what the fuss was about until someone told him that he had just topped last year's record—not bad for a first-timer!

Ray rewarded his aching body with a monster-sized hamburger and a cinnamon bun bigger than the dinner plate it came on. A shuttle bus took him back to his hotel room in Whitehorse. Suddenly back in civilization, he stretched out on his bed and was asleep before his head hit the pillow. Ray dreamed for the first time in his life that his name was at the top of the list.

And this time he wasn't hallucinating.

FOUR

MISSTEPS IN THE DESERT

P ain!

For the next two weeks, Ray couldn't walk, sit up or even reach for a cup of water without his body immediately reminding him of the ordeal he had just put it through. The bottoms of his feet felt like raw meat when he walked on them. His joints creaked like rusty door hinges every time he tried to move. But despite the constant pain, Ray knew he had found a new passion: ultramarathoning. He wanted to relive the moment of triumph he'd felt when he finished the race. Ray was desperate for another challenge.

His runner friend Pat Doyle told him about the Marathon des Sables in Morocco, a legendary race that stretches 243 kilometres (151 miles) across the Sahara Desert. You have to run it in six pre-set stages. Temperatures can climb to nearly 50°C (122°F) at the height of the day and then plummet to near freezing at night. Sandstorms can hit at any time, causing runners to lose their way or even suffocate as they choke on the sand. The terrain is rocky at best, and for at least 20 percent of the race, runners are slogging through soft sand. Once again, participants are expected to carry all their survival equipment on their backs, but in the Marathon des Sables, every item you carry has to be absolutely essential. There are no sleds and no jettisoning is allowed—everything you start the race with must be still with you when you cross the finish line or you'll be disqualified.

Ray began assembling his desert gear. Because of the lack of landmarks in the desert, one of his most important tools would be a reliable compass. It had to be tough enough to withstand the constant jostling and yet remain accurate enough to tell the runner what direction he or she was facing. Clothing was also an important factor. Competitors were advised to bring shorts and T-shirts for daytime running, a hat to shelter their heads from the blazing sun, a scarf to wrap their faces in case of a sandstorm, and a cotton sweatshirt and track pants for the chilly desert evenings. They also had to carry all the food they'd require. (Ultramarathon runners need to consume at least four thousand calories a day.) Ray packed just one type of meal: a dehydrated chicken gumbo that had the highest calorie count of anything he could find. He bought an extremely lightweight stove and enough fuel for a week of running. He also decided to wrap his running shoes with duct tape to ward off the sand. An experienced runner had told him that one of the hardest challenges of desert running was keeping sand out of your shoes. Finally, Ray got vaccinations to ward off polio and typhoid, two diseases that were still common in that part of the world.

As the race date approached, Ray began to train in earnest. He ran five times a week, sometimes as far as 40 kilometres (25 miles) in one day with a full pack. He did speed sprints, where he would run five kilometres (three miles) as fast as he could and then drop back to a jogging speed. It was spring in the Ottawa Valley, and as Ray slogged along the side of the road, the passing cars spraying him with slushy grey snow, he dreamed of clear blue skies and the burning sands of the Sahara.

Finally, it was time to leave. At the Ottawa airport, Ray met a group of people who were also going to race. The slow check-in gave them a chance to get to know one another, and many would become lifelong friends. On the flight across the Atlantic, Ray had a hard time believing he was actually going to Africa. Even after his airplane landed at the Casablanca airport, he still felt as if he were just having a wonderfully vivid dream.

To reach the race camp, the runners first had to make a 277-kilometre (172-mile) connecting flight in a small propeller-driven plane to the city of

Ouarzazate. Strangely, although Ray was born and raised a Canadian, he felt a connection to the sand and rocks below as he flew over the endless desert. What he wasn't prepared for was the heat that hit him and his fellow runners like a wall as soon as they stepped off the airplane.

Taxis took them to downtown Ouarzazate, a beautiful little city of spice bazaars and street-side cafés. The narrow winding streets and square pinkish buildings reminded Ray of a movie set. In fact, Ouarzazate had been used many times as the setting for Hollywood movies, including *Star Wars, The Mummy* and *Gladiator*. After checking their bags at their hotel, Ray and his fellow runners decided to go for a walk through the winding downtown streets. From beneath shady awnings, shop and café owners waved them over and invited them to try their wares.

Ray peeked inside the dark doorway of one shop. The owner immediately invited him in, not to shop but to share tea with his family as an honoured guest. Ray had never tasted tea like this before—it was minty with a great deal of sugar. The shopkeeper seemed fascinated by the fact that Ray had come all the way from Canada just to run across the desert. When the tea was finished, the shopkeeper said he had something for Ray. It was a necklace with a tiny silver ornament called a Cross of Agadez. He told Ray that the cross was a symbol of the Touareg, a nomadic people who have inhabited that part of the Sahara for thousands of years. Although crosses are typically associated with Christians, Touareg Muslims also wear these special types. The centre of the cross is said to represent Allah, the Arabic word for God, and the four points represent the four corners of the world to which people may travel. It was a perfect gift for a person about to spend six days running across the Sahara.

Ray wanted to give something in return. He hadn't brought much money with him, but fortunately he had a spare pair of running shoes in his travel bag. The shoes were a perfect fit for one of the shopkeeper's sons, so the gift was gratefully accepted.

It took three more days for all the racers to arrive at the hotel. When it was finally time to go to the camp where the race would start, Ray picked up his desert survival pack and boarded a large shuttle bus for what he imagined would be a relaxing tourist trip through the desert. Instead, it was a white-knuckle seven-hour ride along narrow and curving mountain roads with no guardrails. When the buses ran out of road, the runners transferred into rugged dump trucks like the ones that usually carry gravel or rocks to construction sites in Canada. The racers protected themselves as best they could as the huge trucks bounced them through the desert like a load of stones.

After an hour of banging around inside the trucks, they finally arrived at the starting camp, which consisted mostly of tents—each one essentially a huge burlap shroud stretched over a tent pole. Ray and eight other Canadians shared a tent. Sleeping spaces were assigned by nationality so that the runners could understand and help one another. Once their gear and sleeping bags were settled in, Ray and all the other runners enjoyed a hearty meal of soup, salad, pasta and fresh French bread.

But Ray was less happy when he lay down to sleep that night. The sleeping pad he'd brought along turned out to be too thin to protect him from the plummeting night temperatures or the rocks on the ground. He woke up the next morning feeling stiff and unrested. "Oh, well," he thought. "Anyone can make one mistake."

The next day was "gear check" day. Ray was nervous that he had either overpacked or underpacked. He didn't want to haul inessential equipment nearly 250 kilometres (155 miles) through the desert, nor did he want to forget some crucial piece of gear that would disqualify him. He was relieved when he was passed by the officials. Now he was officially in the race!

His second night in the desert was as cold as the first, and Ray spent much of it shivering, thanks to his useless sleeping pad. And just as he finally managed to fall asleep, there was a tremendous noise. The camp was like a travelling circus, and each dawn all the tents were pulled down by the Touareg crew, packed up and moved by trucks to the next day's starting point, where everything was set up again. If the racers didn't wake up and get out of the way quickly enough, the crew would roll up the tent with them in it. As soon as the teardown began, everyone had to scramble to grab their gear and get out of the way.

As the tents came down, rock music blared from speakers, interrupted only for announcements about racing information in French and English. After a quick breakfast, the nearly 750 runners were directed by race officials to find their places on the starting line. A gun went off and suddenly Ray was running again in a huge herd, only this time he was running over sun-baked rock and sand instead of snow and ice.

The first day's stage was 28 kilometres (17 miles). For experienced ultramarathoners, this was barely a warm-up. But Ray quickly realized that each day's race had its own unique challenges. If the distance was short, you knew the terrain was going to be extra rugged. If the distance was long, you could expect easier terrain. Some runners were better at hilly terrain, while others excelled at flat-out running. Every runner wanted to complete each stage as fast as he or she could because the final finishing time was the sum of all six stages.

The organizers handed out bottled water at certain checkpoints, and the other runners took these bottles and kept on running. But Ray had brought along two water bottles like the ones he'd used in the Yukon, and he had to take the time to pour the water into his own bottles. He couldn't throw away his bottles because he had to finish the race with everything he'd started with, so he was stuck with them for the whole trip. Mistake number two.

The runners were responsible for their own meals. At the end of the first day, Ray set up his camp, lit his stove and began boiling water to make the first of many meals of dehydrated chicken gumbo. As he looked around, he noticed that few of the experienced runners had a camp stove like his. In fact, most didn't have any stove at all. Instead, they just poured their dehydrated food into a bag of water warmed by the desert sun, shook it and then ate. It wasn't as tasty to eat as food prepared with hot water, but it saved time and the effort of hauling a stove and fuel. Ray realized that he had made another mistake—number three so far, and it was just his first day.

Thanks again to his sleeping pad, Ray woke up stiff and tired the next morning. The pad belonged in the garbage, but the rules required that he carry it all the way to the finish line. This day's run was 34 kilometres (21 miles). Part of it was over sand dunes—the first Ray had ever seen up close—and he felt excited to dip his shoes into a real desert dune like the ones he'd seen in so many movies. Then he discovered mistake number four. Dunes are made of superfine sand. Ray's genius idea of keeping dirt out of his shoes by covering them in duct tape backfired because the fine grit just got under the sticky side of the tape and rendered it useless. Ray's shoes filled with sand and began chafing his skin. He could feel blisters forming, but he kept running. He was passed by an Italian runner who was talking to himself as he ran barefoot through the sand, carrying his shoes in his hands. "Who's crazier, him or me?" Ray thought as he continued to slog along with his sore feet.

He finished the day's distance, but he now had three huge blisters that had to be treated by the race's medical staff. Limping to his tent, he began preparing another gumbo meal. While comparing his dinner to another runner's food package, Ray found out that the calorie count on his daily rations was a manufacturer's misprint. This was serious. Humans need calories from their food just as cars need gas for their engines. Although Ray was eating his fill, he was still losing weight and energy every day. If he became too malnourished, he'd have to drop out of the race. Mistake number five—and he was already sick of the taste of chicken gumbo.

Day four was the dreaded 76-kilometre (47-mile) double-marathon leg. To make things even more interesting, the race organizers had decided that the top fifty runners had to hang back and let the trailing seven hundred have a head start in the morning.

Although the racers were all timed from the moment they started their run to the moment they finished, a late start meant that you had to run in higher temperatures, as well as slogging through sand that had already been roughed up by hundreds of other racers.

With all his mistakes, Ray was sure he was going to be with the seven hundred trailing runners. Instead, he found out he was forty-ninth in the field—just enough to make sure that he had to do this ultramarathon leg the hard way. He felt simultaneously proud to be in the top fifty and downhearted that everything seemed to be working against him. The Old Ray lurked in the background, trying to second-guess every decision the New Ray was making.

"You keep screwing up," the voice said. "You're not going to make it."

Then Ray realized that this race was a unique learning opportunity, and that he should just relax and enjoy the run and not worry about what could have been if he'd had more experience. Hey, he was just a rookie, and yet here he was in the top fifty in one of the world's toughest races. How cool was that?

For the gruelling fourth day, Ray was happy to hook up with two experienced runners who graciously shared their strategy for the day. While most of the other runners in their group rushed ahead, they advised Ray not to panic and just run at his own comfortable pace. "You'll catch up. Don't worry," they said.

Sure enough, as the hours passed, Ray and his companions caught up to most of the other runners one by one. Eventually, Ray began to pull ahead of his new friends. They wished him a good run, and soon, just as he had in the Yukon, Ray found himself running alone, as if he were the only person on earth. But instead of feeling lonely, he felt exhilarated.

Every now and then he would pass through a small village whose inhabitants would stare at him as if he were a fleeting mirage. Dogs barked, goats bleated and small children often laughed and ran alongside him as if they were part of the race as well. Back in the desert, Ray was learning how to read sand the way sailors read water. All sand wasn't the same, he discovered. Some spots were packed hard like a good road, while other spots were loose and slippery like quicksand. If he looked carefully, Ray could see subtle differences in the way the sand was rippled or how it lay beside a curling dune.

Darkness began to descend. Although he'd been running for eight hours, Ray felt a second wind coming on with the cooler night air. With 62 kilometres (39 miles) already behind him for this day, he strapped on his headlamp and began to kick his legs out in longer strides to try to pick up some time. Just six kilometres (almost four miles) from the finish line, his lamp went out, but Ray didn't slow down. Mistake number six.

He ran straight into a sand dune, hitting it so hard he stumbled and fell on his face. Once he got back on his feet, he scrambled up to the top of the dune and spotted the base camp just a few kilometres ahead. It was dark, Ray was very tired and the loose sand made for treacherous stepping. He stepped forward and slipped, tumbling down the reverse side of the dune. When he reached the bottom, the base camp had disappeared. All he could see was another dune in front of him. Ray began to climb again.

For the next hour, he laboriously scrambled his way to the top of dune after dune, only to find that there was always another dune in front of him. Some of the dunes were so steep he had to climb them on his hands and knees. He was exhausted, and he was out of water. Worse yet, he could no longer find the base camp no matter which way he looked because all the race markers had disappeared. It later turned out that some local children had stolen them as a joke, but for Ray and the other runners, this was a serious situation. They were lost in the desert without water at night!

After a few minutes, Ray met a French runner named Karim who was in exactly the same predicament. They spent an hour wandering aimlessly across the dunes. Fortunately, they were eventually found by some race staff driving a support vehicle. These race workers pointed the way to the camp, and Ray and his new friend Karim staggered the last few kilometres to safety. Ray's feet and back were a mass of blisters as he wearily slumped down in the Canadian tent area. Every joint in his body ached, and every muscle felt as if it had been beaten with a stick. Ray was starving, but the thought of yet another meal of lukewarm chicken gumbo made his stomach threaten to walk home on its own. But strangely, Ray felt only happiness and exhilaration. There was no place he would rather be.

The fifth day was a full marathon, but having survived the previous day's ultrarun, Ray felt like he was out for a Sunday stroll. The remaining 20 kilometres (12 miles) of the final-day sprint were even easier. Competing against a field of so many experienced and talented runners, Ray was pleased to cross the final finish line in the top forty. He was even more honoured to learn that he'd placed first among all the North American runners. He wasn't first overall, but he was keeping up with some of the world's best.

FIVE

JAGUARS, TARANTULAS AND BOARS, OH MY!

Maybe it was because of all the training, but Ray's body took much less time to return to normal than it did after the Yukon run. In a week, he was out training for his next race.

Almost immediately, he began wondering what his next challenge would be. Talk about adventure! In just over a year, he had run across the Arctic in sub-zero temperatures and climbed Saharan sand dunes in blast-furnace heat. He was still wondering what else ultramarathoning had to offer when the phone rang. It was Shirley Thompson, one of the first people he'd met at the Yukon Arctic Ultra—the woman who'd thought he was right out of his mind when he told her that he'd never run a marathon before.

Shirley was now organizing her own ultramarathon race, and she'd been so impressed by Ray's enthusiasm (if not his expertise) that she wanted him to take part. She was even willing to waive the entry fee if he could get himself to the starting line.

"Sounds great," Ray said. "Where's the race?"

"The Amazon Jungle in Brazil," Shirley said.

Ray took a deep breath. All he knew about the Amazon was what he'd seen in old movies and TV documentaries. The movies were all about headhunters and streams full of fish that stripped the meat off your bones in seconds. Ray knew that was all silliness. The documentaries were about thick forests of massive trees, umpteen types of bugs and temperatures so high they could nearly cook your brain inside your head. He suspected that these details were true.

"I'm in," he told Shirley.

"Great!" she said, and she told him where and when the race was being held.

The first thing Ray did when he hung up the phone was conduct a little research into the place where he'd be running. He found out that the Amazon Jungle is home to one of every ten animal species living on earth. There are more than 2.5 million species of insects in the Amazon, including thousands of types of mosquitoes, hornets and ants. Piranhas, electric eels, bloodsucking leeches and crocodile-like reptiles called caimans lurk just beneath the surface of its streams and rivers. There are vampire bats that carry diseases like rabies, malaria, yellow fever and dengue fever. There are frogs whose skins secrete a poison so dangerous that natives coat it on their arrow tips when they hunt large animals. There are killer cats like jaguars and cougars. There are wild pigs called peccaries that would lash out with razor-sharp teeth if a runner surprised them on a jungle trail. There are twelve species of poisonous snakes, including deadly coral snakes and bushmasters and constrictors called anacondas that can weigh over 100 kilograms (220 pounds) and would swallow a fully grown peccary in one gulp.

But perhaps the deadliest threat is a danger you can't see—bacteria. Deadly diseases like malaria, yellow fever, hepatitis A and B, and even rabies are easily contracted from insect stings, animal bites or tainted water.

One of Ray's first steps was to visit a doctor, who gave him shots for every disease commonly found in the tropics. While still feeling woozy from his needles, Ray began to assemble his jungle kit. This time it would include lightweight clothes and shoes that would dry fast if he got caught in one of the near daily jungle storms. (They didn't call the Amazon a rainforest for nothing!) Besides food and water, each runner was required to carry a hammock with mosquito netting; a waterproof sheet called a fly to act as a rain shelter; insect repellent; a compass; a knife; safety pins; two glow-in-the-dark cyclaume sticks that would help rescuers find an injured runner at night; a flashlight with spare batteries; waterproof matches or a lighter; an emergency whistle; water-purifying tablets; and a safety kit with salt tablets, painkillers, disinfectant, bandages and tape.

Runners were also encouraged to make sure all their equipment was waterproof. It usually rained at least once a day in the jungle, and the humidity alone could cause non-waterproofed electrical equipment like LED lights and global positioning systems to fail. Once he had assembled his jungle kit, Ray tested it by immersing it in water to make sure nothing would leak.

On the home front, Ray's personal-training business had expanded impressively since his Yukon win. Dr. Duane Smith, whose office Ray had been in when he first read about ultramarathon racing, often referred clients to him for personal coaching. Ray sometimes met these clients in a spare office adjacent to Dr. Smith's. One day, a young blond woman accidentally walked in on Ray and a client while she was looking for the doctor's office. She blurted out an apology. Ray tried to act cool, but he was instantly smitten with her big blue eyes and incredibly cute face.

After she left, Ray begged, wheedled and badgered Dr. Smith's secretary to tell him more about the mystery woman. Eventually, he found out that her name was Kathy and that she didn't have a boyfriend. Ray asked the secretary to give Kathy his phone number. Two weeks later, while he was still wondering about the best way to introduce himself if the phone number didn't work, Kathy called and agreed to meet him for coffee! He felt more nervous than he ever had on the starting line of any race, but within five minutes of sitting down with Kathy, he was completely at ease.

They found they shared a passion for hiking and the outdoors. Kathy had just started running herself, and Ray briefly described his adventures in ultramarathon racing. After their first date, he tried to see Kathy as often as he could, even though he was at the peak of his training schedule.

The race organizers had warned participants that they needed to be in top physical condition to endure the tropical rainforest conditions. They recommended running at least two marathons (a total of 90 kilometres, or 56 miles) a week. Ray ran five days a week, and soon he felt he was ready for anything even the Amazon Jungle could throw at him. But just getting to the race proved to be an adventure in itself.

There was no direct flight from Ottawa to the Amazon. After being seen off by Kathy and his friends at the airport, Ray flew to Toronto, then took a connecting flight to Florida. From there, he flew to São Paulo, Brazil, one of the largest cities in the world. But he had no time to admire the stunning skyscrapers or historic buildings because he had to make a connecting flight to the coastal city of Belém and then catch a midnight flight on a tiny plane up the

Amazon River to a small dirt runway near the city of Santarém. Even at night it was over 40°C (104°F), and the high humidity made Ray perspire heavily while he was just sitting still.

A race organizer took him to a very basic hotel, but the long journey helped Ray sleep soundly through the night. The next day he sampled some local delicacies, including grilled pineapple and barbecued alligator. He was delighted to see that many friends from the Yukon Arctic Ultra were already there. A runner named Jay Batchen asked Ray if he'd be willing to race as part of a four-person team with his friends Kevin Lin and Charlie Engle. Ray readily agreed. He had never met Kevin or Charlie, but he'd heard a lot about them from other runners. Charlie was a television producer with a passion for ultramarathon running. Kevin was a celebrity in his native Taiwan, where he'd been winning races since he was a teenager.

The next day, even though Charlie had yet to arrive from the United States, the runners loaded all their equipment into two rickety old diesel-powered steamboats and set off on a ten-hour trip up the Amazon River. The heat, humidity and fumes from the diesel engine made Ray's head ache. When they reached the camp, they had to climb over the side of the boat and wade through waist-deep water to shore because the river was too shallow for their boats to dock.

Already the heat and humidity were beginning to

make Ray wonder what exactly he'd gotten himself into. Swarms of mosquitoes and other bloodthirsty bugs added to the misery. They were now deep in the biggest jungle on earth, and still no Charlie.

Ray followed the crowd up a steep hill and came upon an amazing site—an enormous base camp cut out of the living jungle by local labour. Two huge shelters had been made of tree trunks and palm leaves. Each one could shield more than a hundred people from the daily rains. Another shelter held hammocks for the racers. The hammocks hung at irregular intervals, depending on where the tree trunks rose out of the forest floor, and each was shrouded in nylon mosquito netting. Ray realized that these primitive-looking beds would be the most comfortable ones he and his fellow runners would see until the race was over.

There was no central lighting, so as soon as darkness fell, everyone put on their LED headlamps to keep from bumping into each other. The runners then had a quick meal and turned in for an early night. On the following day there was a series of equipment checks, route lectures and warnings about the local flora and fauna. It turned out that the birds, bugs and beasts weren't the only danger—there were even plants with poisonous leaves or sword-like thorns that could stab an unwary runner.

The race would be run in six stages over seven days. There would be checkpoints every five to ten kilometres (three to six miles), and any runner who failed to pass through every checkpoint would be disqualified. Time limits had been set for each stage, and any runner who didn't complete a stage in the allotted time would be eliminated. Participants could run individually or as part of a team. Teams had to include at least three members; their official time would be the average of the times of all members combined. All runners had to be self-sufficient, carrying enough supplies to last them for seven days. They also had to carry enough water in their own water equipment, and they had to top it up at every checkpoint in case they got lost.

The last thing the race organizers announced was that the first day's run was only 14 kilometres (8.7 miles). Ray could normally cover that distance in less than an hour, but he knew that the person who'd organized the Yukon route had also designed this race, and that person was famous for setting difficult trails. As he headed back to his jungle hammock, Ray wondered what was ahead of him. Snakes, poisonous thorns or electric eels?

The next day, the runners stepped up to the starting line with their survival packs strapped on. In contrast to the blinding light of the wide-open desert or the soft light of the Yukon dawn, the jungle loomed dark and menacing. The organizers were ready to start the race. And still no Charlie.

Jay, Kevin and Ray had resigned themselves to running as a three-man team when suddenly they heard a roar in the trees. It grew louder. But it wasn't a jaguar or a charging boar—it was an approaching helicopter, one of a pair that Shirley had commissioned in case of emergencies. The aircraft landed with a blast of humid air, and someone jumped off in full running gear.

"Hello, Charlie," Jay and Kevin said as Ray shook hands with his teammate for the first time just a few seconds before the race began. The starting gun went off, and the runners began pounding down the sandy beach toward the first race marker. From what Jay and Kevin had told him, Ray knew that Charlie was a seasoned adventure runner who excelled in this kind of terrain, so he decided to stick to him like a shadow and learn from the best.

Because of their brisk pace, Ray's team and a few Brazilian runners were out in front by the time they hit a wide span of river they had to swim across. The other runners dived straight in, and Ray went in right behind them, even though he wasn't a great swimmer. He emerged last of the leading group on the other side, where the trail went straight into the jungle.

Passing from the sunny beach into the jungle was like being swallowed alive by a living green wall. Within two minutes, Ray realized that the real challenge of this race wasn't the heat or humidity, or even the critters; it was the jungle itself. Roots and vines snagged at the runners' legs, forcing them to constantly look down to keep from falling. But if they looked down for too long, they'd miss the trail markers and become lost. Runners could lose sight of one another in just a few metres of trail.

Ray was barely into the jungle when he realized that he was already off the trail. Fortunately, he remembered what the race organizers had said to do if this happened. He carefully retraced his steps until he finally saw some red flagging tape. Once back on the trail, he ran as hard as he could to make up lost time, but he kept tripping. His shoes were soaked from the swim, and he knew they had no chance of drying in this humidity, so he'd be running with wet feet for the whole day—maybe even the whole race. Wet feet led to blisters. Blisters are painful at the best of times, but in a place like the jungle, they pose a worse threat because they open the skin to infections.

But Ray didn't have time to worry about his feet. The route was more than living up to his expectations for toughness. There were hills so steep that runners had to climb them on their hands and knees. Coming down the other side was equally difficult. Ray mostly slid down on his bum, grabbing the occasional tree branch to slow himself down.

At the bottom of one hill, he splash-landed in a swamp. A thick mist hung over the waist-deep water, and huge gnarled tree roots rose up like sea monsters. Ray had lost sight of all the other runners, so he was glad when a Brazilian runner suddenly slid into the swamp behind him. Neither one could speak the other's language, but they both had the same goal— finding their way out of the swamp. Wordlessly, they waded through the water, half-wondering if some reptile or huge fish was going to drag them under at any second. With a sigh of relief, they finally emerged from the swamp and resumed running. The trail was still rugged, but at least it was land.

A few hours later, Ray and his Brazilian friend straggled into camp together. Three runners had already dropped out of the race, and many of the most experienced runners were calling this day the hardest of their careers. Ray strung up his hammock and draped it with the mosquito net and rain fly. His shoes were still soaked, but the runners had been warned not to walk barefoot because of scorpions. As expected, his feet were beginning to blister. After a quick meal he joined a line of runners outside the medical station to have his feet disinfected and bandaged. Once back under his mosquito net, he was finally able to hang up his shoes to dry and then he slumped like a dead weight into his hammock.

Ray woke up the next morning still tired, partly because of the run and partly because he'd kept flipping over in the hammock in his sleep. More than

once, he'd woken up hanging upside down in the
dark.

That day's run was 24 kilometres (15 miles)—still
just a stroll compared to the distances Ray was used
to, but if the previous day's experience was anything
to go by, he knew it was going to be a battle. The race
began, and again Ray struggled to find a rhythm for
his legs. Vines and roots grabbed at his feet, and the
heat and humidity seemed even worse than before.
Every runner was having his or her own struggles.
The jungle visibility was so limited that Ray soon
separated from the others and found himself running
alone again.

Because of his wet shoes, Ray had a major blister
growing on his right foot. There was nothing he could
do about it in mid-trail, so he made up his mind to
ignore it. Just then, something large rustled behind
him. Immediately, Ray forgot about his foot pain.
Was it a jaguar? he wondered. A bear? Then he saw
a large flash of brown. It was a wild boar! Ray went
into ultra-sprint mode, running down the trail toward
the checkpoint as fast as his legs would carry him. He
could hear the boar's trotters clattering just behind
him. It was grunting and squealing—and gaining!

Ray could see the checkpoint just ahead. He
summoned the last of his strength and made a desperate
dash, shouting, "Wild boar! Wild boar!" to warn the
defenceless people at the checkpoint. He rushed past,

expecting all hell to break loose. Instead, he heard nothing but laughter. He turned and saw the Brazilian volunteers doubled over with hilarity—but no wild pig, which must have turned off the trail just before Ray appeared. To the Brazilians, it looked as though he'd been running away from his own imagination.

The good thing was that Ray realized that if he wanted to, he could actually run faster than he had been. The bad thing was that now his foot was really hurting. When he took off his shoes that night, his feet looked like they belonged to a body fished from a watery grave—they were all white and wrinkly, and his big toe on his right foot had a deep purply shadow. He showed the toe to the camp doctor, who told Ray that he'd developed an abscess in his joint. This was serious. There was no way he could continue running with his toe joint so badly infected, but to treat it the doctor was going to have to cut the toe open and remove the infected flesh. Besides the pain, there was a very real danger of a much worse infection once the doctor opened the skin.

"Do what you have to," Ray told him.

The doctor froze Ray's foot with anaesthetic, cut out the abscess and bandaged the toe carefully. Ray hobbled back to his hammock and tried to get some sleep.

His foot ached badly when he woke up the next morning. But fortunately, all the other runners looked as bad as Ray, if not worse. The camp looked like the site of a tornado or some other natural disaster, with people limping about and covered in mud and scratches.

That day's distance was 31 kilometres (19 miles). Every time Ray hit a puddle or crossed a stream, the water made his blistered feet burn like fire. He thought about quitting constantly, but he reminded himself that he was part of a team. Even though he rarely saw more than a glimpse of Kevin, Jay and Charlie in the jungle, he knew they were depending on him, and that thought helped him throw one foot in front of the other kilometre after kilometre. The Old Ray whispered in his ear, "No one will blame you for quitting. Look at that foot." But the New Ray pushed the voice away. "Forget the feet," he told himself. "This is all in my head."

Ray finished that day's race in good standing, but the next day worried him. It was the longest leg, a real ultramarathon of 85 kilometres (53 miles) that runners had thirty-six hours to complete. They wouldn't even get a full night's sleep because the race was to start at 4:00 a.m. with a swim across the Amazon in full pack and running gear.

Ray's injured foot stabbed him with pain every time he put weight on it, but as soon as the starting gun barked the next morning, he focused on keeping up with his racing companions and the pain faded to the background. Charlie and Kevin were strong swimmers, so they pulled ahead while everyone else flailed and floundered in the water. Ray stumbled ashore with a group of stragglers, and they all got lost as they hit the wall of jungle. Eventually, they found a trail up a steep slope and began to climb. But just as the sun started to penetrate the jungle blackness, a British competitor passed Ray screaming, "Run!" Behind him, Ray heard a strange hum that grew ever louder. Then something stabbed him like a hot needle in the back.

Someone had disturbed a nest of jungle wasps, and they were going after every runner they could find. Everyone ran for their lives. People got stung everywhere. Some of the wasps tried to sting Ray in the eyes, and he received two bad stings in the back and one each on his leg and arm.

The runners finally outpaced the wasps and resumed their normal run. No one had time to nurse their wounds—they had to reach the next checkpoint before early evening or they wouldn't be allowed to continue. They had to check in early because they were now in jaguar country, and jaguars hunted at night. If it looked as if a runner was going to be racing through the jungle in the dark, he or she would be held back until the next morning.

Ray and three other runners reached the checkpoint just in time. They were waved through into a dense, murky jungle that smelled like pee. "That's the jaguars," one of the Brazilian runners said. "That's how they mark their territory. They're out there, only you can't see them."

The jungle was so thick they couldn't really run, so they walked as fast as they could, with their eyes and ears straining for any sign of the killer cats. They were relieved when the jungle began to thin out and the narrow trail they were following widened until it was almost a road. At this point, Ray's companions went on ahead. Ray wanted to follow, but his foot was hurting so much he thought it best to keep to his own pace.

Night began to fall and Ray put on his LED headlamp. Using the tiny light, he picked his way along the trail. At one point he almost stepped on a huge tarantula, but it reared up in terror just as Ray was about to tread on its huge furry head. He managed to pause his foot just long enough for the hairy little beast to dodge out of the way. Ray thought that if he had frightened the tarantula half as much as it had frightened him, it would keep going to the other side of the jungle.

Next, he had to cross a river in the dark. As the little LED light shone into the water, Ray could see the eyes of several caiman alligators close by. He crossed the river in a personal best time and found the marked trail, then turned and began running down a beach. He knew that the next checkpoint was nearby, but he was feeling completely spooked by the jungle. An experienced jungle runner had warned Ray never to shine a light into the jungle at night, but he couldn't help himself. As he ran along the beach, he glanced into the trees—and saw hundreds of eyes of all sizes staring back at him. The jungle was alive!

In spite of the wasps, jaguars, caimans and spiders— or maybe because of them—Ray finished the day in seventh place. They certainly inspired him to keep moving!

The next day, Ray and the lead racers got twenty-four hours off to allow the other runners to catch up with them. Although Ray's muscles appreciated the day off, it also gave his feet a chance to swell, making them even more painful than they were before. But he wasn't going to allow pain to slow him down. As soon as the starting gun fired, Ray was running hard again. Within minutes, he and the other runners were hit by another swarm of wasps, but they kept going. The jungle tripped and tore at them as if determined not to let them go, but suddenly they broke out into broad daylight on a clear beach. They realized that they were into the home stretch.

Most of this leg of the race was a 25-kilometre (15-mile) sprint down the beach, and Ray was determined to get to the end as fast as he could. It felt strange to see signs of civilization again. There were tourist boats out on the water, with people waterskiing and

Running for close to thirty hours you cover a lot of desert— and some beautiful scenery in the Akakus Mountains. *Libyan Challenge, 2006.* (Courtesy Libyan Challenge)

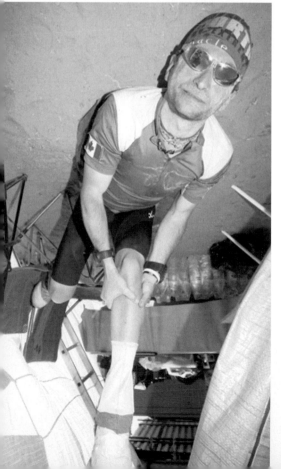

Ouch! Legs are getting crampy. *Libyan Challenge, 2006.* (Courtesy Libyan Challenge)

When the head or side wind really picked up, Ray could only walk while dragging his sled. *Siberian Express, 2010.* (Courtesy impossible2Possible)

After running across Baffin, Ray arrives in Newfoundland to start running the East Coast Trail. *Canada Challenge, 2007.* (Courtesy impossible2Possible)

The youth ambassadors climbing yet another sand dune. *Running Tunisia, 2010.* (Courtesy impossible2Possible)

Communicating live with classrooms all over the world. *Running Tunisia, 2010.* (Courtesy impossible2Possible)

Youth ambassador Sierra makes a friend in the Amazon community. *Expedition Amazon, 2010.* (Courtesy impossible2Possible)

Getting sleep whenever we could between provinces. *Canada ONEXONE, 2008.* (Courtesy impossible2Possible)

Our friends from Gatorade supporting us. *Canada ONEXONE, 2008.* (Courtesy impossible2Possible)

The group makes their way through the Akshayuk Pass. *Baffin Island, 2009.* (Courtesy impossible2Possible)

Ray stops for a break. *Baffin Island, 2009.* (Courtesy impossible2Possible)

Visiting a school in Ottawa before the big trek to the South Pole. *South Pole Expedition, 2008–2009.* (Courtesy impossible2Possible)

Richard Weber and Ray taking a break during the South Pole Expedition. (Courtesy impossible2Possible)

Ray dragging his sled over some jagged snow drifts. *South Pole Expedition, 2008–2009.* (Courtesy impossible2Possible)

A school in California reviewing video from the South Pole Expedition. (Courtesy impossible2Possible)

Ray making a friend in Mali. *Running the Sahara, 2006–2007.* (Courtesy Kevin Lin)

On the home stretch, running on a mining road. *Expedition Atacama Extreme, 2011.* (Courtesy impossible2Possible)

Ray carried his supplies in case of an emergency stop or sleepover in the desert. *Expedition Atacama Extreme, 2011.* (Courtesy impossible2Possible)

sailing. The tourists looked well rested and relaxed. By comparison, the runners—covered in six days' worth of mud, dried blood, thorn scratches and insect stings—looked like a herd of escaped jungle zombies wobbling down the beach.

About five kilometres (three miles) into the run, the pain in Ray's feet disappeared. It was as if pain itself finally gave up trying to make him quit. Now it was only a matter of putting on the pressure. Charlie and Kevin were just ahead of him. They too seemed to find deep reserves, and everyone in the front pack started to feed off one another's energy. Kilometre after kilometre whizzed by. Suddenly, Ray saw a village ahead. There was a series of steps leading up a hill and a banner at the top. Ray ran up the steps, and just like that, the race was over.

Charlie and Kevin had taken first and second place. Ray had placed eighth, and Jay was in the top twenty. As a team, Kevin, Charlie, Jay and Ray took first place. Even though Ray's feet suddenly remembered how to feel pain, he didn't care. He had just run the toughest race of his life, and he was more than just a survivor—he was a winner!

SIX

BACK TO THE SAHARA

PAIN! When his feet were still numb, Ray had managed to hobble through a victory dance or two at the post-marathon celebration party, but by the time he got back to his hotel in the city of Santarém, his feet had swollen up like two angry puffer fish. For almost a week, he was virtually a prisoner in his hotel room, relying on room service for food and bags of ice to pack his feet in. His feet were so inflamed he couldn't put on even his largest shoes, and he needed a cane just to cross the room.

And STINK! He noticed that the bellhops often made a face when they stepped into the room to bring more ice. They peeked around discreetly, as if they suspected that Ray was hiding a dead body in the room somewhere. There were no dead bodies, but he knew why they were looking for one: ever since his week in the rainforest, his feet had given off a rotten jungle smell. Even when his feet were under ice water, people could smell them from across the room.

After a week of ice and rest, however, his feet shrank down enough to allow him to put on his loosest pair of shoes. Ray checked out of his Santarém hotel and began the long journey of connecting flights from Belém to São Paulo, São Paulo to Miami, Miami to Toronto and finally Toronto to Ottawa. All the way home, he kept his shoes laced as tightly as possible and hoped his fellow passengers didn't figure out where the rotting jungle smell was coming from.

Back home, the smell eventually went away as Ray's feet healed, but he unexpectedly developed a worse problem. One day while he was training, he noticed a swelling on the back of his leg. It increased to the size of a fist, and by the time his family took him to the hospital, it had grown to the size of a football. The doctors seemed completely stumped. When Ray told them he'd just returned from the Amazon Jungle and had been stung by a wasp there, they gave him antibiotics and sent him home. But the medicine didn't seem to make a difference. A week later, a second swelling, identical to the first, appeared on Ray's back. Both began leaking a milky pus.

It was disgusting, but fortunately a runner friend named Brian Henderson and Ray's girlfriend, Kathy, were willing to clean and dress the wounds several times a day. (Ray couldn't do it himself because they were in places he couldn't reach.) One day, Brian noticed something poking through the swelling on

Ray's back. "Looks like something is trying to break through," he said. Sure enough, about a day later a lump of slime suddenly popped out, leaving behind a hole so big that Ray could insert his index finger up to the first knuckle. When doctors sent the lump away to a lab, the report concluded it was some sort of parasitic infection that Ray must have picked up from a plant scratch or bug bite in the jungle. Once the parasite was out of his body, the antibiotics finally began to take effect and he started to recover from both wounds. But for months, he had a hole in his back that he had to pack with gauze to keep from leaking.

Undeterred, Ray began thinking about his next race as soon as he was feeling well. While he was in the jungle, Shirley Thompson, the race organizer, had told him about a wild ultramarathon called the Trans 333. Like the Marathon des Sables, it was held in Africa, but it was in the country of Niger, a different part of the Sahara.

The Trans 333 was known for having a variety of terrain that required both running and walking to avoid leg strain. And in this race, runners didn't have to carry their entire supply of food and equipment with them but were allowed to ration it out in "drop bags" that would be waiting for them at prearranged checkpoints. The Trans 333 also differed from the Marathon des Sables and the Jungle Marathon in that there were no daily set stages. Competitors could run for as long as they were able to stay awake or navigate in the desert at night. In the year 2000, a runner named Claude Harde slept for only three of the sixty-two hours it took him to complete and win the race.

Applying to the Trans 333 was like signing up for a secret mission. Ray sent in his forms but didn't hear anything for weeks. Just when he had almost given up, he received a short note from race organizers telling him to fly on a certain date in November to Orly, a major airport in Paris. Ray made his flight as instructed, but when he arrived, none of the airport officials seemed to know anything about a connecting flight to a race in Niger. Everyone he asked just shook their heads and shrugged their shoulders. Ray thought he might have made a wasted trip, but just then, he spotted a group of people wearing running gear and he recognized several French ultramarathon runners from his other races. He asked them if they were going to the Trans 333, they said yes, and the next thing Ray knew he was on a plane to Agadez, the largest city in northern Niger.

As he stepped off the plane onto the bare runway, the dry heat and the desert smell immediately reminded him of Morocco, but he noticed many differences in the architecture and the people. The buildings in Morocco had had a vaguely European look, but here in Agadez they were smaller and made of clay. The inhabitants of Morocco had mostly been medium-built

Arabs dressed in western clothes. The inhabitants of Agadez were mostly Touareg people who wore loose, flowing robes with lots of silver jewellery. Ray self-consciously fingered the silver Cross of Agadez for which he had traded a pair of shoes in Ouarzazate. He didn't know why, but he felt a bond with these people who lived mostly in the desert and made their living bringing trading goods into and out of the region by camel caravans. He had heard that many of the people were extremely poor and that many suffered from diseases. Ray remembered his own battle with infection and parasites from the Amazon, and he was thankful he lived in a country where clean water and free medical care were readily available.

The Niger ultramarathon was called the Trans 333 because organizers took the runners 333 kilometres (207 miles) into the desert and left them to find their way back to Agadez on foot. Someone compared the event to a homing pigeon race with humans. Even by bus and truck, it took two days to reach the starting point, which was a tiny oasis in the middle of the desert called L'Arbre du Ténéré, or the Tree of Ténéré. The oasis was named after the last surviving tree in the Sahara Desert. At one time, much of this part of the Sahara was covered in trees that had managed to sink their roots deep into the sand to draw water from a huge underground lake. But without an adequate yearly rainfall, the water in the underground lake slowly dropped out of the reach of most tree roots. One by one the trees died off, until only this one final one—regarded as a miracle—survived. In 1973, a truck driver, rumoured to be drunk, hit the tree with his vehicle and destroyed it. Now only a metal monument marks the tree's incredible struggle against the odds.

Other than the monument and a few outbuildings, there was nothing in sight but sand. Ray felt a little daunted by the thought of trying to run all the way back to Agadez in such a hostile climate, but he knew he was well prepared. There were fifteen checkpoints between the starting and finish lines. At each one, Ray had stashed a drop bag containing food, water and survival supplies. He had learned a great deal from his many mistakes in the Marathon des Sables, and this time he'd made sure he had exactly the right kind of food and equipment to keep him going.

To keep from getting lost, most runners wore a pre-programmed global positioning system (GPS) strapped to their wrists. In addition, Ray had a good pair of sunglasses, lots of sunblock, a well-fitting pair of running shoes and an MP3 player stocked full of his favourite tunes. When the race began at 4:30 a.m. the next morning, he was raring to go.

Because the race started in the dark, it was pleasantly cool at first. But that did not last. As soon as the sun peered over the horizon, the air began to heat up amazingly fast. As usual, Ray did his best to stick with the most experienced runners and copy what they did. In Niger, there was always a breeze blowing, but that breeze carried with it tiny particles of sand that infiltrated everything and even rubbed the UV layer off Ray's sunglasses as he ran.

The checkpoints were roughly 23 kilometres (14 miles) apart, and Ray rushed through the first couple, pausing only for a quick drink and bite to eat. At the 66-kilometre (41-mile) mark, he got caught in his first sandstorm. There was nothing the runners could do except put their heads down and keep moving and pray that their GPS units didn't choke up. The sand quickly went from ankle-deep to knee-deep, and Ray slogged along as if he were fighting through a burning blizzard. Even with his head wrapped in a scarf, he could barely hear his MP3 over the howling wind and the sound of flying sand smacking against his sunglasses. When the sandstorm ended, Ray suddenly found he was alone. He had no idea where the other runners were. Maybe he was in front of the pack. Maybe he was at the back. Fortunately, his GPS seemed to still be working, so he shook the sand out of his clothes and ears as best he could, cranked up Fatboy Slim on his MP3 player and slogged on.

Ray found the isolation exhilarating. As he ran, he was awestruck by the starkly beautiful desert, which seemed to stretch out endlessly in all directions.

He came from Canada, a land of big spaces too, but the Sahara had a special isolation that made him feel especially alive. Ray was occasionally reminded, however, that the desert was also someone's home.

Every now and then he met caravans of Touareg nomads and their heavily laden camels. The Touaregs smiled and waved, not looking the least bit surprised by the sight of a strangely dressed and sunburned foreigner running alone through the desert like a crazy person. Once he saw a truckload of heavily armed men. They didn't smile and wave, but at least they kept on going, much to Ray's relief.

He occasionally passed small families travelling on their own through the desert. When he stopped to talk to one such family, their little girl kept touching his backpack. He realized that she was interested in the water bottles he was carrying. Unfortunately, one bottle was empty and the other had only a few drops in it. But when Ray gave it to the little girl, her face lit up in a huge smile. She returned to the family carrying the bottle tightly in her hands as if she had just received the best present of her life.

When he reached the next checkpoint, Ray picked up fresh water bottles and explained to the race organizers what had happened to one of his empties so they wouldn't think he'd just thrown the bottle away to save weight. He said he thought the girl probably wanted the bottle as a toy, but the checkpoint officials said it was more likely she was interested in the few small swallows of water. "Clean water is next to impossible to find out here," one of the Touareg guides told him.

As he resumed his run, he was haunted by the image of the little girl desperate for just a few swallows of clean water. "And we just take drinking water for granted," Ray said to himself, thinking of the endless taps of clean water in Canada as he chugged along through the sand.

Ray ran 160 kilometres (99 miles) through deep sand in the first twenty-four hours. Every time he was too tired to go any farther, he would pull out his bivy bag for a quick power nap, the way he had in the Yukon Arctic Ultra. One hazard in Niger that you didn't find in the Yukon was scorpions. Before he could lie down, Ray had to carefully scan the ground for scorpion burrows. If the ground looked scorpion-free, he'd crash for twenty minutes or so and then resume his run.

For most of the time, he rarely saw another human being except for checkpoint staff. Then, at the 230-kilometre (143-mile) point, he saw a Toyota Land Cruiser approaching with one passenger. The passenger was an Italian runner everyone called Max. The poor guy had twisted his knee and had to abandon the race with just the last third to go.

The good news for Ray was that until he'd injured his leg, Max was in second place. Now Ray was second, with only one runner ahead of him. This welcome bit of information gave him a new burst of energy. Suddenly his aching joints and exhausted muscles felt factory fresh again. The desert began speeding by, and Ray passed checkpoint after checkpoint in pursuit of that leading runner.

At the very last checkpoint, just 30 kilometres (19 miles) from the finish line, he was told that if the third-place racer was keeping the same pace as Ray, he was likely only a few minutes behind him. The third runner was a Frenchman named Theo who had actually won the race the year before.

Instead of plunging ahead to try to catch the first-place runner, Ray decided to wait for Theo to catch up so they could run the final sprint together. The Frenchman arrived just as predicted only a few minutes later. When he heard Ray's proposal, Theo also seemed to think that sharing the last leg was a good idea. It was early evening as they set out for Agadez under a clear sky and cooling temperatures. They were both very tired, so they walked as much as they ran. It felt good to Ray to have someone to share these final race moments with.

As the light began to wane they watched the stars come out, and in the distance they could just make out the city of Agadez with its few electric lights twinkling in the hazy air. Not many people living in modern parts of the world can imagine how dark it can get in a wilderness like the Sahara. In a matter of minutes Ray and Theo could no longer see each other, and only the sound of their footsteps kept them in contact. Ray reached into his pack for his headlamp, but to his dismay, he found that the light had died. His GPS was fading fast too. Ray tried adjusting the controls, but the GPS battery was just plain out of juice. Fortunately, Agadez was only a few kilometres away now. Unfortunately, Theo hadn't noticed when Ray stopped to adjust his equipment; he'd kept walking, and now he was gone. Ray was alone in the desert without a light or a GPS. He stumbled his way toward Agadez, guided by the few lights he could see in the distance.

So close and yet so far!

He had run 333 kilometres (207 miles) through the desert and finally reached the city, but in the darkness, Ray couldn't find a way in. Agadez is an ancient city with a high protective wall all the way around it like the medieval fortresses Ray had seen photos of in history books. He ran for thirty minutes along the wall until he finally found a tiny wooden door. He knocked and eventually a man answered. Ray asked, "Can I come in?"

The man answered in a mixture of French and Tamahaq, the language of the Touareg people in that region. Ray explained that he was one of the Trans 333 runners. He wasn't sure if the man understood him, but he seemed to decide that anyone crazy enough to be outside the wall at night and only speaking English probably wasn't a threat to the city. The man opened the door and let Ray in.

He was finally through the wall, but now he had to find his way through the maze-like city streets. Ray just kept running until he stumbled upon the finish line by accident. It seemed like hours, but it was probably only another thirty minutes since he had entered the city. Theo was already there, so Ray had to settle for third when he could have been second. But he didn't feel the least bit upset. He'd run a great race and met a lot of terrific people, and a funny, crazy idea had come into his head that would lead to his greatest adventure so far. Many people had run across part of the Sahara. But had anyone ever run across this huge desert from one end to the other?

SEVEN

HOTTER, DEEPER, DRYER BADWATER

If there was any one place Ray felt most at home, it was in a desert. Scorching dry temperatures didn't seem to bother him, nor did the endless kilometres of sand and rock.

Through his racing friends, Ray heard about another famous desert challenge, the Badwater Ultramarathon, which ran through the famous Death Valley in California. Death Valley is a geologic basin more than 60 metres (200 feet) below sea level. It officially has the lowest elevation, the highest temperatures and the lowest amount of rainfall in North America. With the Rocky Mountains blocking it on all sides from cool, precipitation-laden clouds from the Pacific, Death Valley temperatures can soar to more than 60°C (140°F) in the summer. Less than 40 millimetres (two inches) of rain falls in an average year.

The Badwater Ultramarathon is held every July, when temperatures reach their highest point of the year, and its route crosses the lowest, hottest and driest part of Death Valley. The starting line is at a place actually called Badwater, a flat piece of land where rain occasionally collects to form a brackish temporary "lake" of undrinkable saltwater. Badwater is 85 metres (280 feet) below sea level, making it the lowest place in the western hemisphere. The finish line is at the Mount Whitney Portals, which are 3,962 metres (nearly 13,000 feet) above sea level. The entire race covers 217 kilometres (135 miles), and winds its way up and down three separate mountain ranges. Route checkpoints with names like Furnace Creek, Devil's Corn Field and Stovepipe Wells gave Ray an idea of the kind of conditions he could expect if he signed on.

As a warm-up to Badwater, Ray decided to compete in the Marathon des Sables again. It was the twentieth anniversary of that race, and Ray knew the organizers would work extra hard to make it enjoyable. He also wanted to go back to Morocco to see if he could improve his time now that he'd learned from all the mistakes he made the first time around.

To be able to do his best at both the Marathon des Sables and the Badwater Ultramarathon, Ray asked another runner, Lisa Smith-Batchen, to be his coach. Lisa was the wife of Jay Batchen, his former Amazon Jungle teammate, and was considered a legend in ultramarathon circles before Ray had even begun to run competitively. She'd won many races and had placed first in the female division of both the Badwater Ultramarathon and the Marathon des Sables. To his delight, she said yes.

Although Ray was now a successful athlete and a professional personal trainer himself, he knew he could learn a lot from someone with a running background as extensive as Lisa's. He also knew that she'd push him to even greater feats of endurance. Because they lived thousands of kilometres apart, however, most of their communication was done by telephone. To prepare him for the Marathon des Sables, Lisa insisted that Ray run six days a week—something he'd never done before. At first he doubted that he could even do it, but with Lisa's steady encouragement, he realized once again that any beliefs he had about his own limitations were all in his mind.

Some days, Lisa would have Ray run up and down hills near his Chelsea home for hours to prepare for climbing mountain ranges. Other days, she would have him run long, flat distances to prepare for wide-open spaces. The different workouts developed different muscles in Ray's body, and his performance in both types of terrain improved steadily. But the big payoff came when Ray went back to Morocco for the Marathon des Sables. He again placed first among North American runners, but this time he moved up from the mid-forties to twenty-fourth place overall—an amazing improvement for a runner with only a year's experience.

Once he was back in North America, Ray twice went to Lisa's training camp in Wyoming for some person-to-person instruction. Ray was there as both a student and an instructor. He shared his experience and knowledge with novice runners who were just starting their own ultramarathon careers. At the same time, he was more than happy to learn from the many very experienced ultramarathon runners there, including Marshall Ulrich, a legendary runner and mountain climber. Marshall had already run the Badwater race more than a dozen times, even completing an amazing "quad" in 2001, when he crossed Death Valley four times in one race (twice up and twice down), for a total of 943 kilometres (586 miles). He also ran to raise money for charity.

Ray quickly settled in to the routine of teaching and training at Lisa's camp. Both Lisa and Marshall were very helpful in telling Ray what to expect at the Badwater event. One new wrinkle was that the Death Valley race was on a paved road. So far, Ray had slogged through ice and snow, plunged up to his ears in jungle streams and kicked his way through sand and jagged rocks. Now, for the first time, his feet would be slamming pavement.

Running on a paved road is hard on the feet, and the tar also reflects heat back up at the runner. Because of the extreme conditions, each Badwater entrant was required to have a support team of several people and a pair of vehicles. Ray had no idea how to put together a team like that, but Lisa and Marshall called a few friends, and soon he had a group that included a crew chief named Anton and a nurse named Joanne.

With his team in place and his training complete, Ray was feeling fairly confident. Thanks to Lisa and Marshall, he was more experienced and probably in the best shape of his life. He had also done his homework, learning as much as he could about the race beforehand.

But the months of hard work and preparation seemed to melt away the minute Ray experienced Death Valley's infamous oven-like temperatures. He felt lightheaded just crossing the parking lot from his rental van to his motel room. And he was supposed to run in this? Ray was also a little overwhelmed by the number of famous runners who had turned up to compete. This was going to be a really tough race, he admitted to himself.

The next day began with the organizers lining all the runners up against a towering cliff; a faint line had been drawn near the top to show where sea level was. The starting line was right beside Badwater Lake, which was just a small pool of greenish-grey saltwater. Ray greeted Lisa and Marshall, who were also running that day, as well as the many friends he'd met on other races. It was incredibly hot, but he reminded himself that he was in great shape, well trained and for once didn't have a heavy pack on his back or a sled to pull. Ahead of him was nothing but wide-open road. "Compared to sand, jungle or snow, how tough can that be?" he asked himself.

Because of the added congestion of all the support vehicles, the runners were broken up into groups of twenty or thirty and started off at staggered times. Ray eagerly stepped to the starting line when he heard his group's number announced. When the starter's pistol went off, the runners moved and Ray enjoyed the now familiar feeling of running in a herd. Up ahead were the support vehicles, each one clearly marked with its runner's name. Ray caught up with his team and began knocking down the kilometres toward Furnace Creek, the first checkpoint.

Ray's team shouted encouragement as they handed him water to drink and sprayed him with mist to keep him cool. For the first 27 kilometres (17 miles), he made good time. It was very hot, but he felt strong. His crew chief, Anton, constantly handed him water bottles. Ray drank his fill and kept running.

The second leg of the race was called the Devil's Corn Field, and as soon as he rounded the corner from Furnace Creek, Ray knew why: a sudden gust of unbelievably hot wind hit him like a blast of dragon's breath. It was so hot that he actually laughed out loud in disbelief. But he knew from the more experienced runners that the wind would stop when he reached his next checkpoint, Stovepipe Wells. All he had to do was get there.

Something was wrong, however. The crew member who was monitoring Ray's speed told him that he was slowing down. Ray had also noticed that he hadn't felt the urge to urinate in several hours, even though he was gulping down huge amounts of water. That was often a sign of dehydration. But that was impossible, he thought. He was drinking like a racehorse.

By the time he reached Stovepipe Wells, Ray's legs were cramping. One of his crew gave him a leg massage, but Ray still didn't feel quite right. In other races he'd been dog-tired, footsore and achy in every joint at this point, but this time he felt physically ill.

The next leg was 32 kilometres (20 miles) to a place called Townes Pass. "Just make it to Townes Pass," Ray told himself as he moved forward again. To try to recoup his strength, he decided to walk for a bit before running again. After an hour, he finally felt the urge to urinate. He thought that was a good sign until he looked down and saw that his pee was as brown as syrup and almost as thick. Ray realized that something was seriously wrong.

He told Joanne, the team nurse, what had happened. "Sounds like you're extremely dehydrated," she said. Then Ray began to experience severe leg cramps.

It felt as if the meat was being ripped off his bones by invisible vultures. The pain was excruciating. He thought that if he could just sit down for a few minutes, everything would return to normal. His head was spinning. A fuzzy fog seemed to surround him, and he lost consciousness. When he came to, he was lying on a stretcher in a medical tent.

Ray wanted to resume racing immediately, but he was ordered to drink several bottles of Gatorade to rehydrate his body. The race doctor was worried that he might permanently damage his kidneys if he kept running, so Ray had to provide a urine sample to prove that his body fluids were back to regular levels. When the sample looked normal, the doctor allowed him to return to the race. It was evening now and a little cooler, but the cramps returned as soon as Ray began walking again. His legs became numb, and he started falling down. Despite his crew's encouragement, Ray knew that his body was finished. With tears in his eyes, he informed Anton that he just could not go on.

As they drove back to the race headquarters in the van, Ray replayed the day in his mind. He could not understand what had gone wrong. Never before had he trained so hard for a single race. Never before had he prepared so well, with all the right equipment and even a support crew. And yet for the first time in his running career, he had been forced to quit. Maybe he just wasn't good enough. Maybe the first few races were flukes, and he just wasn't cut out to be an ultramarathon runner. The scariest part was that this wasn't the Old Ray talking—it was the New Ray. Despite all he'd achieved in the Yukon, the Sahara and the Amazon, Ray's self-confidence was gone.

EIGHT

THE CANADA CAMEL

The support team dropped Ray off at the lodge. After a solid night's rest, he could feel his legs again. Even though his heart felt like lead, he asked to be driven out to Mount Whitney so that he could cheer the remaining racers on as they crossed the finish line.

It took all of Ray's self-control to sit through the closing ceremonies, especially as they handed out medals to all the first-time Badwater competitors who'd finished the race. At one point in the proceedings, they read out the names of the runners who had dropped out. Fourteen names were called, but only Ray stood up to acknowledge the polite applause. Just as he used to laugh off being the last person chosen in gym class, he smiled and waved, pretending his pain wasn't there.

After the race, many fellow runners tried to console Ray with their own stories of mistakes made and embarrassing moments. But he just wasn't able to forgive himself so easily. He felt that he'd let down all his friends, family and team members. The Old Ray was back, second-guessing every decision he made and tearing apart every positive thing that had happened since he began his ultramarathon adventure. The worst part was that Ray didn't have a clue why his body had quit on him. Was it possible that he was just not meant to be a long-distance runner?

It wasn't until he had a chance to sit down with Lisa Smith-Batchen that the answer became obvious. After asking a few routine questions, she began to examine the meticulous charts Ray's crew had kept of his water and food intake during the race. She asked Ray if he had swallowed every drop of water his team gave him. Ray confessed that he drank as much as he felt he needed, then dumped the rest to avoid carrying the extra weight. It was just a few ounces at a time, but it had added up.

The truth jumped out at her. The heat in Badwater was so extreme that every precious drop of water counted. Because Ray didn't feel thirsty enough, he hadn't bothered to finish every carefully measured drop in his fluid containers. In all the excitement of the race, none of his team had noticed him dumping his unused water. It was simple: he had sweated out more fluid than he took in. In that extreme heat, he eventually passed a point of dehydration from which there was no way for his body to recover.

Ray felt furious with himself until Lisa told him, "Okay. We all screw up. Learn from what happened." Her long experience had shown her that even the best athletes make mistakes. What separates the successful ones from the failures is their ability to turn a mistake into a valuable lesson. Ray's errors at Badwater could be a gift for future runs, she explained, if he learned never to repeat them.

Once he'd figured out where he went wrong, Ray wanted a chance to prove himself again. Fortunately, just a few days after talking with Lisa, he had a telephone conversation with Charlie Engle, his former teammate in the Amazon race. Charlie had placed third in the Badwater Ultramarathon, and now he and Kevin Lin were planning to run in a new desert race. "It's called Racing the Planet," Charlie said. "It actually takes place in four deserts around the world—the Gobi Desert in China, the Atacama Crossing in Chile, the Antarctic and the Sahara. The first race will be in the Sahara in Egypt. Are you interested?"

As soon as Ray heard the word *Sahara*, his low mood lifted. The Sahara was one of his favourite places, and the prospect of seeing it again from yet another angle was too much to resist. Ray told Charlie that he would love to run. Then Charlie said, "By the way, that crazy idea you had about running across the entire Sahara might actually happen. I can't say anything for sure yet, but I'll keep you posted."

Ray could hardly believe what he'd heard. A few months earlier he had told Charlie and Kevin that someday he'd like to organize an expedition across the entire length of the Sahara Desert. The idea had come to him back while he was running in 40°C (104°F) heat toward the city of Agadez for the Trans 333 race. As he ran, Ray's mind kept wandering back to that little girl asking for a few drops of clean water. Those images still haunted Ray, and it made him want to do something about it.

Ray knew of many runners who competed not just as a personal challenge but also to raise money for charities. He'd heard of charities that raised money to dig wells in places where the local people couldn't afford to buy the equipment and materials to get at the water. Every single well could significantly improve the lives of hundreds of people.

Over the years, various non-governmental organi-zations (NGOs) in the West have been raising money to bring clean water to people living in developing nations. In 1998, Ryan Hreljac, a grade one student in Kemptville, Ontario, learned from his teacher that millions of people were suffering and dying simply because they did not have access to clean water where they lived. To remedy this, Ryan convinced his parents to let him do extra chores around his home to raise money to build a well for one village in Africa. After four months he'd raised seventy dollars, which was

enough to build a well in Uganda. Ryan's extraordinary determination attracted international publicity
and led to the establishment of the Ryan's Well
Foundation, an organization that has since spear-
headed more than 630 water and sanitation projects
in sixteen countries. The lives of nearly three-quarters
of a million people have been vastly improved by this
single foundation.

There's also a charity called H20 Africa, co-founded
by the American actor/screenwriter Matt Damon.
Charlie had been busy organizing the big run, and it
seemed there was interest in filming the proposed
Sahara run to raise awareness about digging wells in
North Africa. As an experienced television producer,
Charlie also knew that he would have to find sponsors
to pay for the equipment, crew and travelling
expenses of such a complicated expedition. One by
one, the sponsors stepped forward, and soon all the
runners had to do was plan when they wanted to run
and where. The thought of being able to fund wells
that would provide water for people like that little
caravan girl made Ray even more determined to run
across the desert. But first he had to complete his little
Sahara race.

The Badwater experience had left him with
lingering doubts about his running abilities. His
body responded well to his training schedule, but
Ray knew that the real battle, as always, was in his

mind. "Running is 90 percent mental—and the other 10 percent is all in my head," he reminded himself every time he felt a trace of self-doubt well up in his mind.

Ray knew that he was at a crossroads. He had to make a lot of decisions that were going to determine the direction of his life for the foreseeable future. He had to choose whether to continue running or accept that it was another dead end. He decided to give it one more try.

He also had to choose whether to ask his girlfriend, Kathy, to marry him. He knew he loved her, and he was pretty sure she loved him, but they both knew that being married to a full-time professional ultramara-thoner would not be easy. Besides the daily training, Ray was frequently away from home for days or even weeks at a time. Would Kathy be willing to accept a married life like that?

To get his answer, Ray one day casually asked her if she felt like going for a hike in Gatineau Park, one of the first places they'd gone when they started dating. Halfway up the trail, a man wearing a tuxedo came out of the woods carrying a tray with a bottle of champagne on it. The man removed a small velvet box from his pocket and handed it to Ray. Inside was a ring. Ray dropped to one knee to ask Kathy to marry him, and she said yes right away.

With his heart feeling as light as the bubbles in his

champagne, he knew he had at least one question settled.

As the race day approached, Ray repeatedly checked his pack, shoes and other gear to make sure that everything was in top condition. He felt fine as he flew from Montreal to Frankfurt, Germany, but on his connecting flight to Egypt, a familiar voice piped up as soon as the Nile River and the sprawling megacity of Cairo came into view. "This is crazy," the Old Ray said. "It's going to be so hot down there, just like Badwater."

Ray felt his stomach clench, but then he remembered that he knew why he'd become dehydrated in California. He had learned from his mistake and would make sure he never did it again. "I'm just going to do my best, and that's all I can do," Ray said to himself. The Old Ray disappeared.

His spirits picked up the second he stepped off the airplane and inhaled the familiar air of Africa. The smell immediately brought back the many good memories he had of Morocco and Niger, making him feel at home. His mood further improved when he saw so many friends at the hotel. More than one hundred runners from around the world were going to compete in this race. Kevin Lin was already there, and so was Marshall Ulrich, from Lisa's training camp. To highlight the international popularity of this race, the organizers had asked each runner to wear a small flag of his or her country, and Ray proudly wore his red maple leaf on his shoulder.

Like the Marathon des Sables, this race was run in six stages over six days. But the course had been laid out by Ian Adamson, an adventure-racing star from Australia who had a reputation for designing some of the toughest courses in the world. The Old Ray tried to surface once more as Ray and the other competitors, some very experienced, climbed on the bus that would take them to the camp at the starting line. "There's going to be some serious butt-kicking," the Old Ray said. Then Ray remembered something Lisa had told him just before he left Canada. "You've trained for this," she'd said. "You're ready."

At the starting line, Ray remembered some more advice, this time from his friend Charlie. "Don't take off fast," he'd cautioned. "Run behind everyone and watch the other runners around you." When the starter's pistol went off, many inexperienced runners lunged ahead as if they were intending to sprint the whole way to the finish line. Ray followed Charlie's advice and ran at his own pace. He turned up the sound on his MP3 player to drown out his own breathing, and soon he lost himself in the music.

One by one, competitors ran out of breath or began bogging down in the sand. But Ray just kept trotting along at his own pace. Soon only Kevin and Ray were left, running side by side in the desert. At the final checkpoint for the first day, with only ten kilometres (six miles) to go, Ray felt so good that he told Kevin he was going to run as hard as he could to see how his body held up. Ray cranked up his tunes and ran. He crossed the day's finish line before the organizers even had time to put up the official banner. "Wow! You ran that really fast," Ian Adamson said in admiration.

That night, Ray's sleep was disturbed by a commotion in Kevin's tent. He went to find his friend fighting off a huge sand-coloured arachnid known as a camel spider. It had probably been attracted to the camp by the runners' lights. The critter was aggressive and fast, and although camel spiders aren't venomous, they can still deliver a nasty bite. They also gave Ray the creeps. For the rest of the race, he checked his tent twice every night to make sure there were no camel spiders trying to crawl into his sleeping bag.

The second, third and fourth days went exactly like the first, with Ray starting off slow behind the other runners but finishing first in the end. Kevin was a close second every time. The fifth day was a dreaded 80 kilometres (50 miles). Ray and Kevin agreed to run the first half together and then finish the day at their own pace. This time, a runner by the name of Joe Holland ran with them until Kevin decided to test him by increasing the pace. Joe stuck with Kevin until they reached the halfway checkpoint.

After a quick lunch and mandatory rest, Joe took

a cooling swim in a nearby water tank, leaving Kevin and Ray to continue the race. Even though Ray could feel his body beginning to ache, he accelerated his pace to make a sprint for the finish line. He was soon by himself again. With just a little ways to go, he saw a huge dune rise up in front of him. It was so steep that Ray had to scramble to the top on all fours, but as soon as he hit the crest, he could see the finish line in front of him.

"Canada Camel! Canada Camel!" the Egyptian crew members called as they saw him loping all alone toward the finish. They had learned that the man coming first every day in their desert was from a faraway land of ice and snow, and in admiration they'd dubbed him the Canada Camel. To the sound of their cheers, clapping hands and pounding drums, Ray crossed the finish line once again in first place, which virtually assured him the top spot overall.

For the final leg of the race, the runners were loaded into Land Cruisers and driven to the edge of Cairo for a ten-kilometre (six-mile) run through the city's crowded streets. Ray found the bustle and noise of the city very distracting. He also found it impossible to keep up with Kevin, who dodged nimbly through the moving traffic and hopped over puddles and garbage in the streets.

As Ray turned a street corner, the Great Pyramid of Giza and the Great Sphinx suddenly loomed large right in front of him. Another runner named Gary was trailing him by a few metres. Ray slowed down and let him catch up so they could finish the race together. As they approached the finish line, an injured Canadian runner named Wade Bloomer stepped forward to give Ray a Canadian flag to carry.

Ray could see Kevin just ahead, standing at the finish line and holding the flag of Taiwan. A huge cheer went up as Ray and Gary crossed the finish line holding Canada's flag. Ray was almost dizzy with happiness. He had come to Egypt laden with self-doubt and minimal expectations, but each day in the desert had only made him feel stronger and more positive about his running. When all the times were added up, Ray was indeed in first place, but winning mattered less than the fact that he'd shed all his fears and worries in the desert. He jumped up and down, hugged his fellow runners and waved the flag again for all to see.

In its nearly five thousand years on earth, the Great Sphinx had probably seen a lot of strange sights pass under its missing nose. It had seen dead pharaohs marched by in priestly processions. It had seen legions of Romans clank by in full armour. It had even seen a little French emperor in a bicorne hat gaze up at its face in wonder. But that was the first time the Sphinx had ever seen a Canada Camel dancing for the sheer joy of being a runner.

NINE

RUNNING THE SAHARA

Ray competed in two more desert races over the next year, and he did very well in both of them. He placed first in a 190-kilometre (118-mile) non-stop race through Libya, and a few months later he, Charlie and Kevin placed first as a team in a race through the Gobi Desert in China, one of the legs of the Racing the Planet marathon. Just after the Gobi race, Ray and Kathy were married. She and Ray had been dating for most of his running career, and she knew the sacrifices required of the spouses of ultra-marathoners. The aches and pains were a challenge, but so were the long absences as loved ones travelled to distant parts of the world to race for a week or more. But Kathy and Ray were about to face their longest separation ever.

One afternoon the phone rang. It was Charlie calling to tell Ray that the big Sahara expedition was on. He'd spent months tracking down sponsors and donors to pay for the supplies, equipment and personnel it would take to organize an incredible trek like this one. Fortunately, as a television producer, Charlie seemed to have friends and connections everywhere.

Still, the logistics of the expedition were mind-boggling. Ray and Charlie were about to run across a desert nine-tenths the size of Canada. No one in history had ever run through the Sahara from one end to the other. The route would cross through six countries. Beginning with Senegal on Africa's west coast, it would go north through Mauritania, east through Mali, east through Niger, north through Libya, then east again through Egypt until it hit the Red Sea on Africa's east coast, a distance of 7,500 kilometres (4,660 miles). Wars prevented them from entering Chad or Sudan, two other countries that bordered the Sahara, and they weren't even sure they'd be allowed to enter Libya because its government was suspicious of outsiders. But if all went according to plan, they would be dipping their toes in the Red Sea as their finish line.

They decided that if they could run nearly double marathons of 80 kilometres (50 miles) every day, it would take them eighty days to cross the Sahara. To accomplish this, they needed a support team to carry their supplies, set up camps and rest stops, and keep them from getting lost in the desert. They asked a writer named Donovan Webster to be their trail boss. Donovan had been to the Sahara numerous times, so he knew the terrain and what to expect. A doctor named Jeff Peterson was recruited to monitor the runners' health along the way and help them if there was a medical emergency. A trip this long would also be extremely hard on the runners' bodies, so Chuck Dale was hired as the expedition trainer/massage therapist. Finally, Mohamed Ixa, a desert expert from the Ténéré region of Niger, was enlisted to be their guide. This four-man team would travel in two SUVs with all the supplies needed to keep the expedition alive and healthy for this ultimate ultramarathon.

Ray and Charlie invited their friend Kevin Lin to join them. The three of them had run as a team several times before, and Ray and Charlie knew that Kevin's iron will would make him an invaluable asset. A final addition to the team was the film crew Charlie had mentioned as a possibility a few months before.

The Sahara Run, as the desert expedition became known, was directly linked to the H20 Africa Foundation, the non-profit organization founded by Matt Damon and Gary White, an engineer turned relief worker. White had been raising money for wells in developing countries for more than twenty years before the Sahara Run was even contemplated. Ray, Charlie and Kevin were happy to run on behalf of such a worthwhile organization. The expedition began on November 2, 2006, at 7:00 a.m. With only the support team, the film crew and a few wild goats as their witnesses, the three runners waded knee-deep into the rolling waves of the Atlantic Ocean and joined hands to cheer the official start of the journey. Then they donned dry running shoes and trotted across a garbage-strewn beach into the crowded streets of Saint-Louis, Senegal, a city on the west coast of Africa.

The three runners looked very out of place as they jogged through the slow-moving traffic, dodging cars, pushcarts and women balancing huge loads of merchandise on their heads. Many people good-naturedly called *"Bonjour!"* to the three strangers as they ran past. Ray, Charlie and Kevin smiled and also called *"Bonjour,"* which was all the French they knew. As they passed the city limits, suddenly the Sahara stretched before them as far as the eye could see. One of the expedition's two SUVs accelerated ahead to set up the first rest stop, many hours away. The three runners settled into their stride and began to clock the first of the thousands of kilometres they would cover on this trip.

The sun was setting when they reached the Senegal–Mauritania border. Ray's nose detected a hot meal nearby, but the sight of their tents and sleeping bags set up and waiting for them was equally welcome. After devouring a quick hot meal of rice and spicy stew prepared by their African crew, the runners dragged their weary bodies off to bed. In the darkness, they drifted off to sleep listening to Charlie's new ending for the Good Night, Sleep Tight rhyme: "Don't let the scorpions bite."

Scorpions were just part of the danger. By day, the Sahara looks devoid of life because most animals hide in cool burrows to escape the desert heat. At night, however, millions of insects, mice and small lizards leave their burrows to forage for food. And when these critters come out, so do the animals that hunt them. Spiders, snakes, scorpions and other nocturnal hunters prowl the desert in search of prey. Many of these hunters have poisonous fangs or stingers. Although they wouldn't deliberately seek humans to attack, they would sting any unwary person who accidentally stepped on them or lay his or her sleeping bag on top of their burrows. Thanks to modern medicine, scorpion, spider or snake stings are rarely fatal, but they are extremely painful and can make a human very sick for weeks.

The first day's run had been a relatively relaxed 35 kilometres (22 miles) to allow everyone to shake themselves and their equipment out. Day two was the beginning of a gruelling routine that would require them to run at least three times that distance to cross the Sahara in the planned eighty days. A typical day started at 4:00 a.m., long before the sun was up. To take full advantage of the cool morning air, the team would begin running with LED lights clipped to their hats. When the sun appeared the temperature soared quickly, and by 11:00 a.m. they were forced to stop because the heat exceeded 50°C (122°F).

During breaks, they stretched out in the shade of their support vehicles while Chuck, their trainer, poured water over them to cool them off and Dr. Peterson checked their feet for blisters and foot fungus. Besides the heat rash and blisters, in Mauritania they were sometimes plagued by swarms of flies that covered them from head to foot and even crawled over their food as they ate. They tried to catch some sleep, but even in the shade it was like trying to sleep in a sauna.

The run would resume around 5:00 p.m. for at least four more hours. The exhausted runners would then eat their fill, crash into their sleeping bags and sleep until 4:00 a.m. the next morning, when they started all over again. It made for a total of twelve hours of running per day.

They repeated this routine every twenty-four hours, often running a daily double marathon or more. When they stopped, they usually drew crowds of curious locals. If it became known that there was a doctor in the expedition, people would line up for medical attention, and Jeff would share the expedition's meagre supplies of ointments and antibiotics. The first ten days were especially challenging. Both Ray and Kevin suffered from stomach problems and diarrhea. All of them had twisted ankles from the rough and rocky roads, and their hands and ankles were swollen from the constant jogging motion. But somehow their spirits remained high.

They played mental games with themselves to take their minds off their aching bodies. One day, Ray played the same fourteen-minute rock song by Peter Frampton twenty consecutive times on his MP3 player just to get himself thinking about the music, not his feet.

By day 17 (November 18), the Sahara team had already completed twenty-five full marathons. Chuck joked that the runners had now reached their "maximum stink" because their clothes and their bodies were so soaked by weeks of perspiration they couldn't absorb any more. They used their precious water only to wash their hands before eating and their feet at the end of a day's running. In their entire expedition, they would enjoy only two showers. Because he was physically smaller than Ray and Charlie, Kevin just could not drink enough water or Gatorade to prevent dehydration on some of the longer days, and Dr. Peterson had to administer IV bags of saline water to ease his aching muscles.

On day 39 (December 10), they reached eastern Mali, 2,579 kilometres (1,603 miles) into their run. Just over the border, they encountered a seven-year-old boy living by himself in the desert with only a dog and a small goat for company. His parents were on a weekly quest for water, which was a two-day trip each way. It was a reminder to everyone that this run was more than just a personal challenge.

On day 44 (December 15), they crossed into Niger. By day 54 (December 25), Ray and Charlie had lost more than 18 kilograms (forty pounds) each, and the much slighter Kevin had lost a proportionate 11 kilograms (24 pounds). They looked like running skeletons, and they were still only halfway through their race. They were each consuming more than 900 litres (240 gallons) of water and sports drinks a month, or about four times Ray's own body weight in fluid every week.

On day 64 (January 4, 2007), a sandstorm hit. They put on long-sleeved clothes and goggles to protect themselves from the wind, which was blowing sand into their faces at 80 kilometres per hour (50 miles per hour). It was hard to breathe, and the sand particles felt like needles against their skin. The vehicles became stuck, and precious time and energy was expended pushing them out. The sand clogged their ears and nostrils, and they could feel grit in their teeth. Even their shoes filled with sand. At one point the sand was blowing so hard that they lost sight of the support vehicles. Even their tire tracks were swept away. With their lives depending completely on a satellite hundreds of kilometres overhead and two little batteries in their wrists, they kept running blindly through the storm until the hunched shapes of their tents appeared as if by magic in front of them.

On day 74 (January 14), they passed a green flag wired to a battered oil drum, which marked the Niger–Libyan border. So far they had run 108 marathons, and they still had more than 1,400 kilometres (870 miles) to go. At the border they met Omar Turbi, a Libyan American businessman who had finally obtained permission for the expedition to pass through Libya only the day before. But their route was now complicated by the fact that the Libyan government insisted the expedition avoid any areas near military bases or oil wells. Instead of their own vehicles, the runners had to follow Libyan security Jeeps, which zigzagged up and down winding side roads. By the end of each day, they had usually advanced only 25 kilometres (16 miles).

By day 80 (January 20), the day they'd planned to finish the race, they were only passing Tripoli. They still had more than 1,000 kilometres (620 miles) to go. It was frustrating. It was cold and windy for most of the Libyan run. They ran past still-active minefields left behind by the German and British armies in World War II, and everywhere the smiling face of Muammar Gaddafi, Libya's strongman leader, beamed down at them from billboards.

On day 100 (February 9), they finally crossed the Libyan–Egyptian border. Egyptian security cars replaced the Libyan ones, but from now on the runners decided the route, not the police. Although they were way behind schedule, their spirits and their speed picked up as they ran on well-paved Egyptian roads and were encouraged by applauding locals who'd heard about the three runners who had already crossed 6,400 kilometres (almost 4,000 miles) of the desert.

Despite their worn bodies, the three began to set new records for running, averaging 80 kilometres (50 miles) per day. By day 108 (February 17), they had run the equivalent of 166 consecutive marathons. But the paved roads and higher speeds took their toll physically. Charlie developed a blister the size of a baseball on one foot, and the whole team had to slow to his limping pace. Although the finish line was so close, the run had ceased being an adventure and had turned into a nightmare that never seemed to end.

The team's spirits picked up again on day 110 (February 19) as they reached Giza. To his delight, Ray saw his old friends the Great Pyramids and the Sphinx suddenly appear through the foggy morning haze. They had now run 7,275 kilometres (4,520 miles). Despite their exhaustion and broken bodies, they decided to run the last 160 kilometres (99 miles) in one go because Charlie's foot seemed to get worse every time they took a break. They were worried that if they paused for a rest, Charlie might have to drop out and the race would end with the finish line almost in sight.

They ran through the cool night wearing long track suits and LED lights. By dawn on February 20 they were in the middle of Cairo, a city of sixteen million people, and it seemed like most of them were sharing the road with Charlie, Ray and Kevin as they limped along the highway shoulder. Horns honked constantly, but the drivers were smiling and waving.

Finally the smell of saltwater and desert slowly replaced the city stink of engine exhaust and stale garbage. They were into the home stretch. At the beginning of the race, only a few feral goats had watched the team wade into the Atlantic Ocean, but now a small army of Canadian, Taiwanese and American supporters walked beside the three runners as they approached the Red Sea. Their closest friends and family members had flown in from all around the world to be with them as they completed their amazing adventure.

At last the road ended. Now a deserted beach studded with folded umbrellas and empty chairs was all that separated them from the Red Sea. Everyone stopped 10 metres (33 feet) from the water to let the three battered runners walk across the sand alone.

On the count of three, Kevin, Ray and Charlie reached down and touched a small rippling wave as it rolled up the beach. When the water touched their hands their incredible journey was officially over—an adventure that had taken 111 days, covered 7,500 kilometres (4,660 miles) and was equal to 170 marathons without a day off.

After a few hundred hugs and handshakes and a toe dip or two in the sea, it was time to go. Ray was looking forward to his first shower in a couple of months, some rest, a good meal and above all some time alone with Kathy.

Then he heard a voice. It wasn't Charlie. It wasn't Kevin. It was the Old Ray, but with a new attitude— and this time the voice asked, "So what are we going to do next?"

TEN

NEXT STEPS

R ay, Charlie and Kevin had hoped the Sahara Run would bring a little publicity to the lack of potable water in North Africa, but they had no idea that their lonely adventure would change their lives. Almost as soon as their weary hands dipped into the Red Sea, reporters from around the world began calling to ask about the expedition and the three runners who had completed it. The publicity helped focus the world's attention on what can be done to help people find clean water. Since the Sahara expedition, H2O Africa and its sister organization, Waterpartners, have brought clean water to more than 142,000 people in Africa, Central America and South Asia.

After the publicity died down, Ray and his wife, Kathy, joined the board of directors of the Ryan's Well Foundation, and they continue to support its mission of bringing clean water to people in developing countries. The Sahara Run also convinced Ray that any future expeditions would need to unite the physical

goal of running a challenging route with an "awareness" goal that would help make the world a better
place. He had barely shaken the Sahara sand from his
running shoes when he launched his next adventure.
In August 2007, he organized his own ultramarathon,
the Canada Challenge. Ray's physical goal was to run
extremely rugged trails along all three of Canada's
ocean coastlines. His awareness goal was to promote
an organization called Spread the Net, a charity that
donates bed nets like the one he'd used in the Amazon
Jungle, to children in places where malaria kills
thousands each year. Each net can save children from
becoming sick or even dying from malaria and other
diseases caused by mosquitoes and other biting insects.

Using a camcorder, a computer and the Internet
to record his experiences, Ray made it possible for
people around the world to watch him prepare his
equipment and run his trails. On August 22, 2007,
he began by running 100 kilometres (62 miles)
along the Akshayuk Pass on Baffin Island in Canada's
Nunavut territory. Three days later he was in St.
John's, Newfoundland, to run 220 kilometres (137
miles) along the Atlantic Ocean. And on August 29 he
travelled to Vancouver Island to run a 75-kilometre
(47-mile) ultramarathon along the Pacific Ocean
shoreline. As Ray had hoped, hundreds of mosquito
nets were purchased and donated to Spread the Net
through a link on his website.

He could hardly believe that just thirty months separated the day he started long-distance running and the day he finished the Sahara Desert expedition. In every case, the physical challenges had been incredibly hard, but the real struggle had always been in Ray's head. He realized that the Sahara Run was like a metaphor for life. Often a problem seems impossible to solve because it is just too big, too long or too complicated, like the desert itself. Yet even the toughest problems can be cracked if you have faith in yourself and persevere.

In 2008, Ray became interested in working with teenagers to help them learn to surpass their own perceived limitations and realize that they have the power to make positive changes in the world. He founded impossible2Possible (i2P), a non-profit organization that combines the latest Internet technology with amazing real-life adventures. Teenage participants called ambassadors find themselves hiking and running in some of the most extreme environments in the world, and as they run, they keep in direct contact with fellow students around the world using laptop computers linked with satellite Internet. The students can ask questions about what it's like running and hiking in faraway places like the Arctic or the jungle. In return, the ambassadors describe what they've learned about both themselves and the world we all share. Since its founding in 2008, i2P has taken ambassadors to Baffin Island, Tunisia, the Amazon, and Bolivia. More expeditions are planned for the future.

"The expeditions are a neat way for my ambassadors to realize, just like I did, that what they think are their limitations are merely self-imposed fears in their heads," Ray says. "As soon as the ambassadors discover their own freedom from limitations, they pass the message on to other young discoverers who are following their adventures on the impossible2Possible website."

In January 2009, Ray and two other Canadians (Kevin Vallely and Ray's old friend Richard Weber) set a world record for walking to the South Pole without external support. During that expedition, Ray used the latest satellite technology to communicate with i2P students around the world and answer their questions about what conditions were like. In 2010, Ray and Kevin also trekked across the frozen surface of Lake Baikal in Siberia to again raise awareness for clean drinking water and to further promote the i2P experience.

Ray still can't believe how running has transformed his life. If someone had told him back in his smoking days that he'd soon be running the Sahara Desert or walking to the South Pole, he would have said they had the wrong guy. But by learning to challenge his own self-imposed limitations, Ray is living proof that anyone can change his or her life through hard work and determination.

"I'm just a regular guy who up until a few years ago totally underestimated what I felt I was capable of," Ray says. "Since then, my experiences have taught me that we are *all* capable of the extraordinary in our lives. I hope that you find your passion and work very hard to make your dreams come true."

RAY'S RACES AND EXPEDITIONS

Ray's Races 2004 to 2007

Yukon Arctic Ultra (Yukon, Canada): 160-kilometre (99-mile) non-stop—1st place (2004)

Marathon des Sables (Morocco, Africa): 250-kilometre (155-mile) stage race—top North American each time (2004 and 2005)

Trans 333 (Niger, Africa): 333-kilometre (207-mile) non-stop—3rd place (2004)

Jungle Marathon (Amazon Jungle, Brazil): 200-kilometre (124-mile) stage race—1st place team, 8th place solo (2004)

Racing the Planet Sahara (Egypt, Africa): 250-kilometre (155-mile) stage race—1st place (2005)

Libyan Challenge (Libya, Africa): 190-kilometre (118-mile) non-stop—1st place (2006)

Racing the Planet Gobi (Gobi Desert, China): 250-kilometre (155-mile) stage race—1st place team (2006)

Ray's Expeditions 2007 to 2011

Running the Sahara: To raise money to build wells in Africa, Ray, Kevin Lin and Charlie Engle ran 7,500 kilometres (4,660 miles) from Senegal to Egypt. Ray and his teammates ran an average of 70 kilometres (43 miles) a day for 111 consecutive days through six countries. (November 2006 to February 2007)
www.runningthesahara.com

Canada Challenge: To raise awareness for Spread the Net, Ray ran along the coastlines of Canada's three oceans. He ran a total of 395 kilometres (245 miles) along Baffin Island, Newfoundland's east coast and British Columbia's west coast. (August 2007)
Visit www.rayzahab.com for info.

Canada ONEXONE Expedition: To raise awareness and support for a Canadian-based humanitarian organization called ONEXONE, Ray and a team of runners ran an average of 80 kilometres (50 miles) a day for thirteen consecutive days, with each run taking place in a separate Canadian province or territory. (May 2008)
www.canadaonexone.com

South Pole Expedition: Ray, Richard Weber and Kevin Vallely speed-walked 1,100 kilometres (684 miles) to the South Pole, setting a new world-record time of 33 days, 23 hours and 55 minutes. The trek took them from sea level to 3,050 metres (10,000 feet), and the team endured temperatures of −40 degrees. (December 2008 to January 2009) www.southpolequest.com

Baffin Island: Ray and five youth ambassadors from across North America trekked the Akshayuk Pass in Canada's Nunavut territory. In just under eight days, they travelled 100 kilometres (62 miles) in High Arctic conditions. During their trek, Ray and his ambassadors learned about Inuit culture and climate change. They also shared their experiences with more than five thousand students who tuned in via satellite technology from schools across Canada and the United States. (September 2009) www.impossible2possible.com/world

Siberian Express for Water: To raise awareness about the need for potable drinking water in developing countries, Ray and Kevin Vallely ran 650 kilometres (404 miles) over the frozen surface of Lake Baikal in Siberia. Lake Baikal is the world's largest and oldest lake, and it contains 20 percent of the world's supply of surface fresh water. Ray and Kevin averaged 50 kilometres (31 miles) a day while hauling all their

own supplies and food. (March 2010)
www.siberianx.com

Running Tunisia: Ray and four i2P youth ambassadors ran 260 kilometres (162 miles) through the North African desert in Tunisia. They endured sandstorms, scorching temperatures and endless sand dunes. Using the Broadband Global Area Network (BGAN), they kept in contact with ten thousand students from around the world. The students raised $30,000 for two water projects in Africa. (April 2010)
www.runningtunisia.com

Expedition Amazon: Ray, two Team i2P members and four i2P youth ambassadors ran 120 kilometres (75 miles) through the Amazon Jungle. They learned about biodiversity and indigenous cultures, and communicated by videoconferencing with sixteen thousand students around the world. (October 2010)
www.jungle2010.com

Expedition Atacama Extreme: Ray ran the length of the Atacama Desert, a 1,200-kilometre (745-mile) stretch that runs from Peru to the Copiapó region of Chile. He averaged 60 kilometres (37 miles) a day over some of the hottest, driest and rockiest terrain he's ever been on, completing the trek in twenty

days. Through his impossible2Possible website, thousands of students around the world were able to follow Ray's adventures as he ran along trails once used by the Chasquis, the legendary messengers of the Incan Empire. (February 2011)
www.atacamaextreme.com

Expedition Bolivia: Five incredible youth ambassadors ran 200 kilometres (124 miles) across the high Bolivian Altiplano in one week. Once again, a comprehensive and interactive educational program was a key part of the expedition. This time the topic was chemistry—scientists on the expedition analyzed the biochemistry of the runners and even brought live chemistry experiments from the Altiplano to classrooms around the world. (May 2011)
www.bolivia2011.com

ACKNOWLEDGMENTS

I would like to thank Eric Walters, a great friend, for his inspiration to write this book.